A Question Of

Tides

(A Tidal Enigma)

D J Haskell

Dedicated to Jenna Isobel Niamh Byrne, a very much loved and greatly missed granddaughter, affectionately known as 'Bubb' who sadly passed away after a heart transplant operation at the tender age of 21 years on 16th May, 2018.

One of Jenna's favourite spots was the small Welsh seaside village of Llangrannog, which lies on the coast of Ceredigion looking out across Cardigan Bay with its dolphins, porpoises, seals and occasional sunfish.

At very low tides along the coast of Cardigan Bay the remains of once enchanted ancient Welsh woodlands are revealed, although the tides hold no secrets now for our beloved 'Bubb' - every wave that caresses the sands on the incoming and outgoing tide triggers fond memories - with nature showing that the spirit of our beloved Jenna is still amongst us.

Acknowledgements

Without having read a book, titled, Prisons of Light, it is highly unlikely that this book would ever have been written, and therefore I owe the author, Kitty Ferguson, a depth of gratitude and many thanks for her easily understandable explanation into the fundamental mechanics behind the tides.

I would also wish to thank Paul G. Hewitt whose excellent book titled, Conceptual Physics, Sixth Edition, further deepened my understanding of not only tidal forces but that of centrifugal and centripetal force. A book on physics I would recommend to any person interested in the subject.

Last but not least an appreciation and a thank you to Paolo Sirtoli and his online explanation (see below) relating to tides and centrifugal force. His words are music to my ears and I quote, "At many websites, but also in some textbooks, one finds plainly wrong explanations of the lunar and solar tides. In particular much confusion arises when authors try to explain the existence of the second tidal bulge, the one opposite to the Moon. Often they invoke the centrifugal force as an 'explanation'. But centrifugal force is a fictitious force, and we can't justify a real effect with a fictitious force, can we?" end of quote.

Prisons of Light (Black Holes) by Kitty Ferguson, Cambridge University Press, ISBN 0-521-62571-8.

Conceptual Physics (Sixth Edition) by Paul G. Hewitt, HarperCollin*Publisher*s, ISBN 0-673-39847-1.

Tides and centrifugal force by Paolo Sirtoli.
www.vialattea.net/maree/eng/index.htm.

Wikipedia, the free encyclopaedia.

Daily Telegraph, Buckingham Palace Road, London, SW1W 0DT, (www.telegraph.co.uk).

Daily Mail, Northcliffe House, 2 Derry Street, London, W8 5TT, (www.dailymail.co.uk).

Meteorological Office.

YouTube.

The numerous journals, magazines, books and electronic media I have read that have contributed to my knowledge during research into this subject.

THE TRUTH IS OUT THERE

King Cnut (Canute) the Great (995 – 1035)

PREFACE

There are few people who can correctly explain how the tides operate and to exacerbate the situation many sources claim the tidal bulge on the side of the Earth furthest from the Moon is due to centrifugal force. This is arrant nonsense and no doubt the following words will seem rather puzzling, but put simply, the tides on our planet are due to the Earth falling towards the Moon and to a lesser extent, due to the Earth and Moon system falling towards the Sun. There is absolutely no need to employ the term centrifugal force in an explanation of the tides and it is indeed rather puzzling to do so. Hence the books sub-title, 'A Tidal Enigma', as many books and websites, even in the 21st Century, persist in perpetuating such erroneous information - hopefully this book will, in everyday language, clarify the situation for the reader.

The Bristol Channel experiences the second highest tidal range on the planet; the highest tidal range is attributed to the east coast of Canada in the Bay of Fundy. Measurements have recorded a maximum range of 16.3 metres (53 feet) with a highest predicted extreme of 17 metres (56 feet). This high tidal range is due to its shape, bathymetry and distance from the continental shape.

You would think that people living on or near the coast with the threat of floods and coastal erosion would be motivated to a greater degree to learn of the forces that could potentially threaten their homes and lives.

Considering the east coast and the nation's capital city, on the 8th May, 1984, the Queen officially opened the Thames Barrier to protect London from flooding.

London's vulnerability to flooding was highlighted by the North Sea flood of 1953, in which over 300 lives were lost in Lincolnshire,

Suffolk, Norfolk and Essex. The official report into the flood was instrumental in the construction of the Thames Barrier.

The gates of the barrier help to regulate the flow of water in the Thames, which is a tidal river all the way to Teddington Lock in south west London. The barrier stops tidal surges from flooding large parts of London, as well as during periods of high flow in Teddington Weir.

The Thames Barrier cost just over £500 million to build and spans 520 metres (1,706 ft) across the river Thames at Woolwich Reach, in south east London. The barrier is composed of 10 gates, which are raised monthly for testing, and was constructed between 1974 and 1984 to protect London from flooding during exceptionally high tides; the gates are closed about four hours before the peak of the incoming surge tide is due to reach it, the trigger point being when a combination of high tides forecast in the North Sea and high river flows at the river's tidal limit at Teddington Weir would exceed 4.87 metres (16 feet) in central London

Moving from the east coast to the west of the British Isles one can witness the second highest tidal range on the planet in the Bristol Channel, with a range of about 15 meters (50 feet). The Severn Estuary with its funnel shape, tidal range and underlying geology of rock, gravel and sand, are responsible for strong tidal streams and a high level of turbidity which gives the water a notably brown coloration as can clearly be seen in satellite images.

It should be noted that the high ground of Exmoor and the south Wales Mountains have the effect of funnelling the predominantly westerly winds increasing the wind speed. The relatively low friction of the water surface will also increase the wind speed as it moves across the water, such that waves are formed and a mass of water will be moved up the channel causing an increase in tidal range.

During 1607 a deadly flood hit the shores of the Bristol Channel drowning thousands of people as houses and villages were swept away; farmland was inundated and much livestock was destroyed.

The Welsh side of the channel suffered from Laugharne in Carmarthenshire to Chepstow on the English border, being badly inundated – even today there are still plaques on churches that survived the flood indicating how high the flood level rose - some up to more than eight feet above sea level.

There is, for example, a small brass plaque on the north wall inside the parish church of Saint Mary Magdelene, Goldcliff, near Newport, Gwent, indicating the flood waters rose to about 0.9 metres (3 feet) above the ground.

On the English side of the Bristol Channel the coast of Devon and the Somerset Levels were flooded as far inland as Glastonbury Tor being 23 kilometres (14 miles) from the coast. Many villages were affected in Somerset – over 70 per cent of the houses in Brean were destroyed with 26 people dying and the Church of All Saints at Kingston Seymour was flooded to a depth of 5 feet with many other churches being inundated to a depth of up to 2.4 metres (8 feet).

The cause of the Bristol Channel flood is still disputed between two possible causes such as a combination of weather extremes and tides (storm surge) that caused the devastating floods during 1953 in East Anglia, or that of a tsunami. It has been suggested the tsunami was triggered by a landslide off the continental shelf between Ireland and Cornwall, or that an earthquake along a fault system in the sea south of Ireland was the cause – the jury is still out as they say.

CONTENTS

INTRODUCTION

Considering we are an *Island Race* with the Bristol Channel experiencing the second highest tidal range on the planet coupled with the fact that it was not so long ago that we had the largest and most powerful navy in the world - including a large merchant fleet - it is truly enigmatic (some would say shameful) that hardly anyone in the British Isles can adequately explain how ocean tides occur except to opine it is something to do with the Lunar cycle. Indeed how many people appreciate there are also land tides, and atmospheric tides.

During a full tide the Earth experiences an ocean tidal bulge on the side of the Earth facing the Moon with a further tidal bulge at the same time on the other side of the Earth facing away from the Moon. These bulges are increased when the Moon and Sun are in line when facing the Earth – the Sun's gravity adding to that of the Moon and these are the highest tides known as Spring Tides.

But how do we experience a tidal bulge on the Earth's surface facing away from the Moon as there is apparently no upward gravitational force to pull on the ocean? Indeed it can be argued there should be no bulge as the strength of the Earth's own gravity should easily hold the mass of the waters to the surface of the Earth.

In discussing such matters as the tides, many people confuse centrifugal and centripetal force. There is no need to mention either of these forces in explaining the tides, but in doing so many people become confused and as a consequence start talking nonsense. Physicists will tell you that a centrifugal force arises due to an object in rotation, but it is not a 'real' force in the sense of the four fundamental forces of physics such as gravity, electromagnetic, weak nuclear or strong nuclear forces – as such centrifugal force is known as a 'fictitious' or 'psuedo' force.

Although a centripetal effect is called a force it is fundamentally a generic term given to any centre seeking force that keeps an object moving along a circular path. Examples of a centripetal force being the force of gravity that keeps a satellite and the International Space Station in orbit, or a planet in orbit around a star such as the Earth around the Sun, or the Moon in orbit around the Earth.

Gravity is a force of attraction between masses. A moving object will continue to move in a straight line at the same speed unless a force acts upon it. Thus for an object to move in a circle, a force has to act on it all the time, and gravity is the centripetal force that keeps the planets orbiting the Sun and satellites around a planet.

Likewise if you swing a ball about your head at the end of a piece of string, it will follow a circle as centripetal force is provided by the string acting as a centre seeking force – if the string should suddenly snap then the ball would fly off at a tangent to the circle due to inertia and not due to what is referred to as a centrifugal force. It is important to recognise that the ball does not fly off suddenly due to a 'new' force acting on it, but because a real force (the string) has suddenly stopped pulling the ball to the centre of the circle – the centripetal force has gone and the ball continues in a straight line as a tangent to the circle due to the principles of inertia,

This book explains tidal forces without the use of formulae, complex diagrams or mathematics. But to placate the mathematically minded or those seeking qualification to the assertions in the book, appendices have been included - those readers having a thorough knowledge of basic physics being able to skip chapter one, and start at chapter two.

Have an enjoyable and enlightening read – trusting that at the end of your journey you will be able to impress friends and folk with your newly found knowledge.

CHAPTER ONE

SOME BASIC
UNDERSTANDING

Before getting down to the nitty gritty, as they say, a bit of basic physics can save a lot of confusion in discussing the forces behind the tides. So it is worth reminding ourselves of some fundamentals about the tides and that of some physics; hoping this will clarify any possible misunderstanding or misconception readers may already have.

I feel this is necessary as a lot of people, including those who should know better in the scientific community, have a misconception of what is referred to as a centrifugal force – indeed, many websites and text books are woefully wrong in their understanding and explanations of the so-called centrifugal force as we shall see in this book.

We will do all this without referring to unnecessary formulae, complex diagrams or mathematics – the following is not rocket science and we will, start with the tides.

Tides

During a full tide the Earth experiences an ocean tidal bulge on the side of the Earth facing the Moon with a further tidal bulge, at the same time, on the other side of the Earth facing away from the Moon. These bulges are increased when the Moon and Sun are in line when facing the Earth – the highest tides, known as Spring Tides; occur around the time of a New and Full Moon. That is when the Sun, Moon and Earth are in direct alignment - the Sun's gravity adding to that of the Moon.

When the Moon is at right angles to the Earth and the Sun, then we have what is known as Neap Tides - the Sun and Moon's tidal influence are virtually at right angles during the first and last quarter of the Moon. As such the ocean tides have their lowest amplitude.

Mass

Mass is the amount of material (matter) in an object. Matter is anything which occupies space and is classified into solids, liquids and gasses. The greater the mass of an object the greater is its inertia (its resistance to change). Therefore mass is the tendency of an object to resist being moved, or if it is moving, to resist a change in speed or direction.

Mass is measured in kilogrammes: The standard unit of mass, the kilogramme, is a block of platinum preserved at the International Bureau of Weights and Measures in France. The kilogramme equals 1,000 grams. A gram is the mass of 1 cubic centimetre (cc) of pure water at a temperature of 40 degrees Celsius. (It should be noted that the standard pound is defined in terms of the standard kilogramme; the mass of an object that weighs 1 pound is equal to 0.4536 kilogrammes).

A mass of 1 kilogramme will have a weight (force) of 9.8 newtons (2.2 pounds) acting upon it at the surface of the Earth due to gravity

Weight

The downward force that results from the gravitational attraction of the Earth to bodies on its surface is called weight. It is directly proportional to the mass of the body and the mass of the Earth, decreasing inversely proportional to the square of their distance apart. To put it more succinctly weight is the 'force acting upon an object due to gravity'. Thus an astronaut will experience different weights on celestial bodies of different mass. For example, on the Moon, which has less mass than the Earth, the gravitational force is only 1/6 as strong as on the Earth. Thus a person weighing 80 kilogrammes on Earth will only weigh approximately 13 kilogrammes on the Moon.

Weight is measured in newtons; the unit is named after Sir Isaac Newton (1642 – 1727). It should be noted that in 'everyday usage' weight really refers to the mass of a person or object. That is why people, when asked their weight, reply in kilogrammes, (or stones, pounds and ounces).

The difference between mass and weight must be clearly understood.

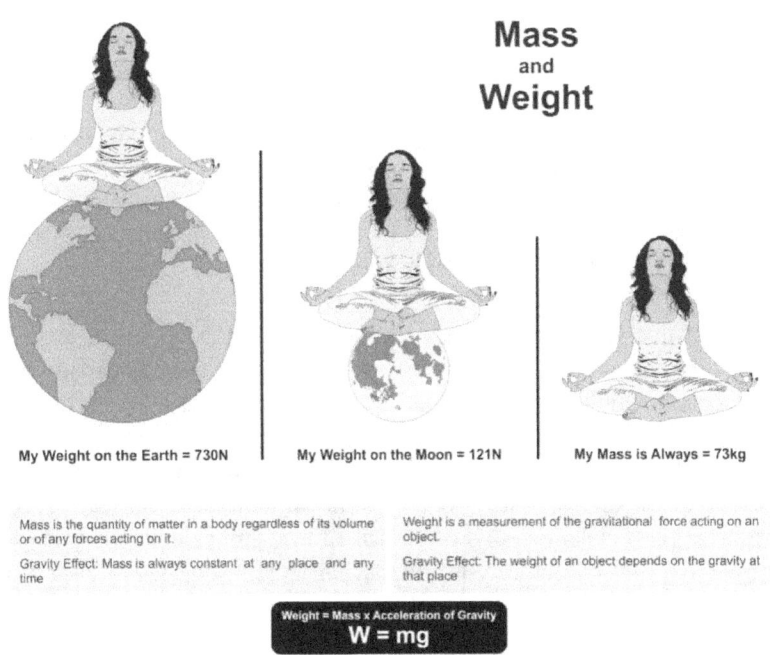

Mass
and
Weight

My Weight on the Earth = 730N | My Weight on the Moon = 121N | My Mass is Always = 73kg

Mass is the quantity of matter in a body regardless of its volume or of any forces acting on it.

Weight is a measurement of the gravitational force acting on an object.

Gravity Effect: Mass is always constant at any place and any time

Gravity Effect: The weight of an object depends on the gravity at that place

Weight = Mass x Acceleration of Gravity
W = mg

Weight will vary dependent upon the mass of the bodies. Weight is a force and will be different on different celestial bodies of different mass, but the mass of an astronaut will remain the same. Mass is the quantity of matter in a material body. The astronaut offers the same resistance to speeding up or slowing down regardless of whether the Earth, Moon, or anything else that is attracting him.

For example: In a spaceship located at a point between the Earth and the Moon, where gravitational forces cancel each other, the astronaut still has mass - if he were to stand on a scale, he would not weigh anything, but his resistance to a change in motion is the same as on Earth. As a further example it must be recognised that it would take the same push (effort) to start moving a vehicle on a level surface on the Moon as it would on the Earth, but it would require much more effort to lift the vehicle on Earth that it would on the Moon. The extra effort is required because of lifting the vehicle against the force of gravity. Mass and weight are very different from each other.

Force

A force is a push or pull upon a body resulting from the bodies' interaction with another body. Whenever there is an interaction between two bodies, there is a force upon each of the bodies. When the interaction ceases, the two bodies no longer experience the force. Forces only exist as a result of an interaction.

So, what is a force? Scientists will not be able to explain it, as they do not understand the nature of force themselves. They know of only the effects, which is either a push or a pull produced by a something they call a force. They also postulate that forces always occur in pairs such that when you sit on a chair the weight of your body presses down on the chair. At the same time an equal upward force from the chair balances this downward force - physicists also do not know what gravity actually is and can only claim that it some kind of pulling (attractive) force inherent to all masses.

Forces can exert a push or pull at-a-distance despite their physical separation, and it is productive to remind ourselves of the gravitational, electrical and magnetic forces.

The fundamental forces (or fundamental interactions) of physics are the ways that individual particles interact with each other. It turns out that for every single interaction observed taking place in the universe can be broken down to be described by only four types of interactions: Gravity, Electromagnetism, Weak Interaction (or Weak Nuclear Force), and the Strong Interaction (or Strong Nuclear Force).

Gravity – is a purely attractive force and reaches through even the vacuum of space to draw two bodies (masses) toward each other. It is instrumental in keeping the planets in orbit around the Sun and the Moon in orbit around the Earth. Of the fundamental forces, gravity has the farthest reach but it's the weakest in actual magnitude.

The Sun and planets exert a gravitational pull on each other despite their large spatial separation – when you jump in the air and you are no longer in contact with the ground, there is a gravitational pull between you and the Earth.

Electromagnetism – electromagnetism is the interaction of particles with an electrical charge. Charged particles at rest interact through electrostatic forces, while in motion they interact through both electrical and magnetic forces.

For a long time, the electric and magnetic forces were considered to be different forces, but they were finally unified by James Clerk Maxwell in 1864, under Maxwell's equations. Electromagnetism is perhaps the most obviously prevalent force in our world, as it can affect things at a reasonable distance and with a fair amount of force.

Magnetic forces - are at-a-distance forces - two magnets of unlike poles can exert a magnetic pull on each other even when separated by a distance of a few centimetres. They can also exert a repulsive force, such that like poles of a magnet repel each other.

Weak Interaction - the weak interaction is a very powerful force that acts on the scale of the atomic nucleus. It causes phenomena such as beta decay. It has been consolidated with electromagnetism as a single interaction called the "electroweak interaction." The weak interaction is mediated by the W boson (there are actually two types, the W^+ and W^- bosons) and also the Z boson.

Strong Interaction - the strongest of the forces is the aptly-named strong interaction, which is the force that, among other things, keeps nucleons (protons and neutrons) bound together. In the helium atom, for example, it is strong enough to bind two protons together despite the fact that their positive electrical charges cause them to repulse each other. In essence the strong interaction allows particles called gluons to bind together quarks to create the nucleons in the first place. Gluons can also interact with other gluons, which give the strong interaction a theoretically infinite distance; although it's major manifestations are all at the subatomic level.

Newton's Universal Law of Gravitation

Newton's law of Universal Gravitation states that every mass in the Universe attracts every other mass with a force that for two masses is directly proportional to the product of their masses and inversely proportional to the square of the distance separating them.

The greater the mass of two masses then the greater the force of attraction between them - the greater the distance of separation, then the weaker the force of attraction.

It should be noted that the force weakens as an inverse-square law. The inverse-square law is a law relating the intensity of an effect to the inverse square of the distance from the cause. Gravity follows an inverse-square law, as do the effects of electric, magnetic, light, sound and radiation phenomena. Since the force of gravity decreases as the square of the distance, a planet twice as far from the Sun is pulled toward the Sun with a quarter the force; three times as far, a ninth and four times as far, a sixteenth and so on. Thus the pull of gravity diminishes very quickly with distance and if plotted graphically would follow an exponential curve.

Inertia

Newton's first law (Principle of Inertia) states that all bodies preserve their state of rest or their state of uniform motion in a straight line, except in so far as it is made to change that state by external forces. Now every material object possesses inertia: how much depends on the amount of matter in the substance of the object. Inertia (inertial force) is measured in newtons within the metric system, (it should be noted that in the imperial system the unit of force was measured in pounds). We frequently meet examples of the inertia of matter in daily life. If you are standing up in a train, which suddenly starts to move forward you fall backwards because some force urged your feet forward.

But the upper part of you, not being acted upon by a force, tended to remain still. If you are standing up in a moving train, which suddenly stops you fall forward for a similar reason. Jumping off a moving bus in the same direction as the bus is moving can be deemed dangerous, unless you deliberately throw your body backward, in order to land in a forward slanting position when you reach the ground. The inertia of a flywheel keeps an engine running smoothly.

Some bodies have more inertia than others; in other words, it is more difficult to start them from rest or stop them in motion. It is easier to push a small car rather than a lorry along a level road; the reason for this is because there is a greater quantity of matter in the lorry than in the small car. In other words the mass of the lorry is greater. This is not to be confused with the weight of the lorry as we are not trying to lift it.

Therefore the greater the mass of a body the greater will be its inertia. Indeed, some scientists regard inertia as just another form of mass.

Barycentre

Most celestial bodies are symmetrical in that they are spheroid and the centre of mass is at the geometric centre of the body (See appendix 5).

Thus a freely rotating body will always rotate about an axis passing through its centre of mass. Now two or more bodies, such as a multiple star system or a star and its accompanying planets, will have a common centre of mass. Binary stars orbit about their common centre of mass, which in astronomical terms is known as the Barycentre.

If two stars of the same mass are gravitationally linked then they will orbit equally about their common centre of mass. If one of the stars is greater than the other, then the common centre of mass is shifted towards the more massive star. If one of the stars is sufficiently massive enough then the common centre of mass will reside within the larger star; this is exactly the situation with the Earth and the Moon.

The mass of the Earth at 6×10^{24} kilogrammes is far greater than the Moon at 0.0735×10^{24} kilogrammes; indeed it is 81 times as more massive. So the centre of mass for the Earth, Moon system lies within the Earth itself.

Thus the Moon's orbit is far more obvious and observable about the barycentre than that of the Earth: whilst the Moon orbits about the Earth at an average distance of 3.84×10^{8} kilometres and this is easily observable; the Earth in effect wobbles about its axis and in the same context this motion is far from discernable.

Free Fall

Isaac Newton compared the motion of the Moon to a cannon ball fired horizontally from a top of a high mountain. He imagined the mountain top to be above the Earth's atmosphere, so air resistance would not slow the motion of the cannon ball.

When the cannon ball was fired with a small horizontal velocity, it would follow a parabolic (curved) path and soon fall to the ground due to the effect of gravity. If more gunpowder were to be used the ball would be fired faster and its path would be less curved thus hitting the ground farther away.

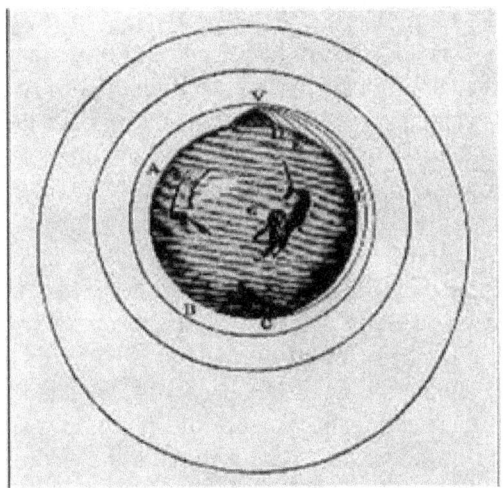

"The greater the velocity...
With which (a stone) is projected, the
farther it goes before it falls to the earth.
We may suppose the velocity to be so increased, that it would describe an arc of
1, 2, 5, 10, 100, 1000 miles before it ar-
rived at the earth, till at last, exceeding
the limits of the earth, it should pass into
space without." - Isaac Newton, *System of
the World.*

If the cannon ball were fired fast enough, Newton reasoned, the projectile would travel so fast as to never hit the ground. The parabolic path would become a circle and the cannon ball would circle the Earth indefinitely – in other words, it would be in orbit.

Newton's first law of motion states that an object in motion tends to stay in motion in a straight line unless acted upon by some force. Thus the cannon ball in this example travels in a curve around the Earth only because Earth's gravity acts to pull it away from its straight-line motion – and, of course, gravity is acting as a centre seeking force that we call a centripetal force – see centripetal force later in this book.

The cannon ball is effectively falling around the Earth in the same manner as the Moon. The Earth's gravity pulls it toward its centre, but the Earth's surface curves away from it at the same rate at which it falls. Both the cannon ball and the Moon have 'sideways' velocity, or tangential velocity parallel to the Earth's surface, which is sufficient to ensure motion around the Earth rather than into it. If there is no resistance to reduce their speed, the Moon and cannon ball 'fall' around the Earth indefinitely.

It should be clear that when the astronauts in a NASA space shuttle are floating about in Earth orbit, they are not doing so because they are too far away to be affected by the Earth's gravity. It is because the downward acceleration of the spacecraft cancels the pull of the Earth's gravity. The orbiting spacecraft is falling and its orbital motion causes it to fall around the Earth the same as the cannon ball.

This is also the reason why the International Space Station (ISS) never hits the ground as its horizontal speed means that by the time it has fallen, for example, 1 metre, the ground is 1 metre farther down due to the Earth's surface being curved - so effectively, the ISS is perpetually falling, but never getting any closer to the ground.

We are all aware of the sensation we have in a lift (elevator), if it is rising fast you can detect the pressure or force on your feet by the floor of the lift. But if it is falling rapidly you will experience a lightness of feeling with perhaps an uncomfortable feeling in your stomach. These are due to the effects of acceleration and deceleration.

If we take this a step further and imagine you are in a box similar to a lift high above the surface of the Earth; in fact the box is in space but still within the influence of the Earth's gravitational field. If the base or floor of the box is facing toward the Earth and the box is stationary with respect to the Earth's surface your senses will detect a force holding you to the base of the box. This you will assume is natural and due to gravity.

Should this box suddenly plummet towards the Earth as fast as falling objects accelerate towards the Earth (at an acceleration of 9.8 metres per second per second), then you will suddenly find you have no weight. If you push against the floor you will find yourself floating about in the box like a feather in the wind. If the box plummeted towards the Earth with a far higher acceleration, then you would find yourself pressed toward the inner surface of the box furthest from the Earth; that is, the ceiling of the box.

I hope from this explanation you can see that from inside the box the sensations due to gravity (due to the Earth's mass in this case) or acceleration are the same.

The experience of being in free fall (zero gravity) is amply shown in videos on YouTube when the late Professor Stephen Hawkins, Professor of Mathematics, Cambridge University, became the first person with a disability to experience weightlessness in a zero-gravity inducing flight in 2007. The professor flew in a modified Boeing 727 which after climbing to about 33,000 feet, then descended rapidly for about 8,000 feet and for the next 20-30 seconds everything in the aircraft is weightless.

A similar aircraft is used by NASA to train astronauts. The usually fit and young NASA astronauts involved often refer to their own zero-gravity aircraft as the Vomit Comet, because of the regularity with which they lose their lunch to its stomach-churning manoeuvres.

Now imagine you are in a stationary spaceship, with no means to see outside, far out in inter-galactic space and far from any gravitational body. Since the spaceship is at rest and there is no gravitational body to influence your environment, you will be in a state of weightlessness since weight is what you call the force with which a large mass pulls on an object. Thus you will find yourself bobbing and floating about the spaceship. Now when the spaceship starts to accelerate in the forward direction relative to the distant stars, you will find yourself pushed back towards the rear of the spaceship. You will, in a sense, have a force of gravity.

Now when the spacecraft decelerates, you will find yourself thrust forward in the same way that people are in any conveyance, which is speeding up or slowing down on Earth. When the spaceship comes to rest again you find yourself bobbing and floating about again. Your body and brain will tell you (from your everyday experience of motion) that the spacecraft was motionless initially, then it accelerated forward, then it slowed down again, then it stopped.

To continue with this theme let us imagine you and a number of fellow space passengers are now travelling along in a spaceship with a constant velocity relative to the distant stars. Suddenly a stray and massive celestial body narrowly misses the rear of your spaceship, but inside the spaceship nobody is aware of the near miss, as there are no windows to look out.

The passengers will feel they are being pulled back into their seats as the celestial body passes them by. The mass of the body has imparted a force on them all... But since they were not aware of the presence of the celestial body and since the effect is the same as if the spaceship had accelerated, all the passengers will assume the spaceship had accelerated and carry on with whatever they were doing before the event.

Thus the passengers have no way of determining whether they are being subjected to a pull from a passing mass or undergoing acceleration. Now it is easy to comprehend that a spaceship experiencing acceleration is in motion. But when the spacecraft is subject to the effect of a gravitational field the concept of actual motion is not apparent.

It should be noted that the concept of 'zero gravity' is a misnomer for gravity is everywhere in the Universe. When astronauts float about in the International Space Station they are in fact plummeting toward the Earth inside the space station. But luckily for them they keep missing the surface and are in orbit travelling sideways at many thousands of kilometres per hour, thus effectively falling around the curvature of the planet. The impression that gravity is not present is an illusion due to their weightlessness, and if the Earth's gravity suddenly disappeared the space station would hurtle away into space at a tangent to the surface at about 28,000 km/h (about 17,000 mph).

The force of gravity obeys the inverse square law which means that any two objects feel a gravitational attraction that is inversely proportional to the square of the distance between their centres. To put it more simply if we double the distance we travel from say the Earth; then the pull of gravity will be four times weaker. If we triple the distance from the Earth, then the gravitational attraction is nine times weaker. No matter how far we travel away the Earth's gravity is always there, but of course, it is imperceptibly weaker.

Newton's First law of Motion

It is very important to remember Newton's First Law of Motion which simply states that a body in motion will remain in motion unless it is acted upon by an external force. For example, if a massive body is moving through space in a straight line, its inertia will cause it to continue in a straight line unless an outside force causes it to speed up, slow down or change direction.

Newton's Second Law of Motion

Newton's second law of motion describes the relationship between an object's mass and the amount of force needed to accelerate it. Such that the FORCE acting on an object is equal to the MASS of an object times its ACCELERATION.

Newton's Third Law of Motion

For every action, there is an equal and opposite reaction. Such that as gravity causes you to exert a force on the ground; the ground appears to exert an equal and opposite force on your feet. When you are accelerating in a vehicle you appear to exert a backward force on the vehicle seat - as we shall soon see that in a rotating system, a centripetal force pulls a mass inward to follow a curved path, while the mass appears to push out due to its inertia. In each case there is only one real force being applied, whilst the other is only an apparent force!

CHAPTER TWO

CENTRIPETAL AND CENTRIFUGAL FORCE

Centripetal Force (a generic term)

I trust the reader will forgive the repetition in this chapter, but due to the misinformation, indeed errors found in many text books (that should know better) and also on numerous websites the intention is to press home exactly what is meant (or not meant) by a centripetal or centrifugal force - hopefully clearly distinguishing these forces, (or more accurately effects), from that of inertia and Newton's first law of motion. In anticipation I thank you dear reader for your patience and hope your tolerance will be rewarded.

Actually there is no such thing as a centripetal force - centripetal force does not exist in its own right, but is provided by the action of other forces and the wording is a generic term for any inward force keeping an object in a circular path such as the force of gravity keeping the Moon in orbit around the Earth, or whirling a conker on a piece of string around in a circle - the centripetal effect (force) is the result of tension within the string.

Sir Isaac Newton mentioned the term centripetal force (*viscentripita*) in discussions of gravity in his 1684 *De Motu Corporum*, stating a centripetal force is that by which bodies are drawn or impelled, or in any way tend, towards a point as to a centre.

A body in uniform circular motion undergoes a centripetal acceleration, and according to Newton's second law of motion, a force is required to produce this acceleration. In the case of an orbiting planet, the force is gravity. The gravitational attraction of the Sun has an inward centripetal effect on Earth. This effect produces the centripetal acceleration of the planets orbital motion.

A force is needed to maintain a body in an orbit of constant speed, at each instant, the velocity of the planet is tangent to the orbit. In the absence of gravity, the planet would obey the law of inertia (Newton's first law of motion) and fly off in a straight line in the direction of the velocity at constant speed. The force of gravity serves to overcome the inertial tendency of the planet, thereby keeping it in orbit.

Centripetal means 'centre seeking' or 'toward the centre' and as such a centripetal effect is any force that causes an object to follow a circular path. Examples are electrical and gravitational forces: The orbiting electrons in atoms experience an electrical force toward the central nuclei. It is a centripetal effect, i.e. the gravitational force of the Sun that keeps the Earth in orbit around the Sun. If this force should suddenly fail then the Earth would shoot off into space at a tangent to its orbit at approximately 107,320 kilometres per hour, (66,700 mph). It should be clearly understood that the current term, centripetal force, is not a separate force as such, but a generic term for all centre seeking forces causing circular motion.

The planets of the Solar System travel around the Sun in circular orbits, or more correctly, elliptical orbits. The Earth's orbit is almost circular - whilst Mercury and Mars are the most elliptical. In order to follow a circular path without changing speed, a continuous force must be continuously applied at right angles to its path. The Sun's gravity provides this force as a centripetal effect for the planets.

As mentioned above, the current name, centripetal force, is a generic name for *any force that keeps an object moving with a uniform speed along a circular path.* The gravitational pull of the Earth's gravity on the Moon being a good example - or that of a piece of string connected to a ball being whirled around your head - to keep the ball whirling above your head two forces must act on the ball – we do not pull the ball directly towards ourselves, but effectively to one side, whilst the string stops the ball flying away resulting in rotation above our heads - thus our arm muscles give a force of motion to the ball, whilst the string imparts a centripetal effect on the ball to keep it moving along a circular path.

Remember also when an object is following a circular path, its velocity is changing all the time - if the velocity is changing, it is accelerating, even if its speed is constant.

Summarising and to reiterate yet again, it is very important to realise that the current term, centripetal force, is a GENERIC term for all centre seeking forces. A piece of string has the ability to exert a centripetal effect, so has a car safety belt, gravity, or magnetism; for a vehicle turning a corner, the centripetal effect is provided by friction between the tyres and the road surface.

Centrifugal force (a fictitious force)

Any outward force that is attributed to circular motion is called a centrifugal force whereby centrifugal means centre-fleeing or away from the centre.

No doubt ardent supporters of a centrifugal force will claim the Bible tale of David and Goliath; 1 Samuel 17:49 (King James Version) which records, 'And David put his hand in his bag, and took thence a stone, and slang [it], and smote the Philistine in his forehead, that the stone sunk into his forehead; and he fell upon his face to the earth' is a perfect example of centrifugal force at work with a stone being released from a slingshot (shepherd's sling) by David.

Unfortunately it would be a false claim as the Biblical tale simply demonstrates inertia (first law of motion) at work - there is no such thing as a centrifugal force; it is imaginary and something physicists refer to as a fictitious force.

There is a lot of misunderstanding to the nature of centrifugal force. A good example again is of whirling a ball around your head. We know that a force keeps the ball following a circular around your head. Note that you have to pull to keep the ball in circular motion; the faster you get it to go around in a circle, the harder you need to pull.

But should the string suddenly snap, it is incorrect to say the ball would shoot straight away at a right-angle to the circle. This is a common misconception as when the string breaks, the ball will actually follow a straight-line path at a TANGENT to the circle, due to the fact that the force provided by the string has suddenly ceased, and only a force of motion acts on the ball and thus INERTIA prevails. It is totally wrong to say the ball flies away due to a centrifugal force.

Quite simply it is due to the principles of inertia that causes the ball to fly off at a tangent to the circle - so why make up a false force – in the case of the ball, centrifugal force is not a 'new' force but just another name for inertia and if some wish to retain the word centrifugal, then the term should more correctly, be called a CENTRIFUGAL EFFECT.

Now imagine you are a passenger sitting in the front seat of a speeding car and are not wearing a seat belt. An animal suddenly leaps into the road directly ahead of the car causing the driver to slam on their brakes. The braking throws you forward against the dashboard hurting your ribs as if some invisible force slammed you against the dashboard. But the reason you slammed against the dashboard was not due to an additional force (centrifugal) hurling you forward, but because of the absence of a seat belt holding you back. Your body is simply obeying the law of inertia, wishing to continue your forward motion in the car.

Imagine you are in the same car and again not wearing a seat belt when the car suddenly rounds a very sharp corner to the left. This time you will find yourself being thrown to the right of the car against the car door not because of an outward force acting on your body, but because there is no centripetal acting on your body to hold you in a circular motion – wearing a seat belt would provide the necessary centripetal effect – your body is again simply obeying the law of inertia. It is very important to recognise that the idea of a centrifugal force throwing us against the car door is a misconception.

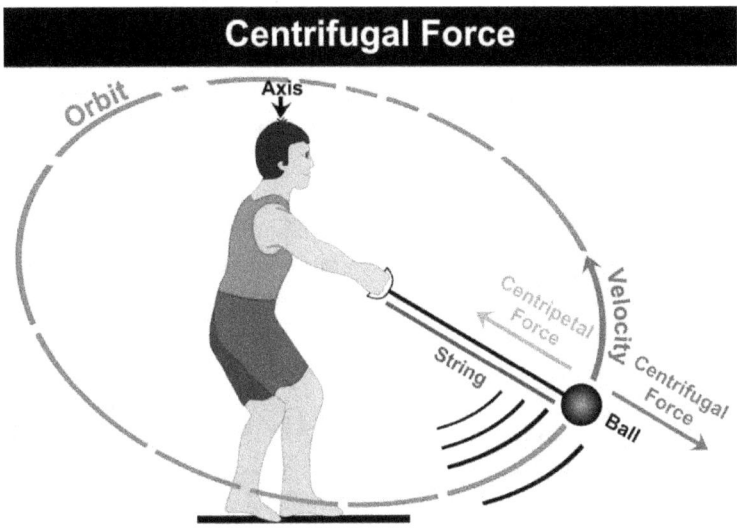

Centrifugal Force

We are all familiar with the carnival show, the Wall of Death, where a motor bike rider hurtles around the inside of a large wooden cylinder of about 10 metres in diameter. Inside the cylinder, the motorcyclist rides along the vertical wall of the cylinder and performs various stunts while doing so. So what is happening and why does the bike not fall off the wall? A lot of people will say it is due to a centrifugal force (to fly outwards) and friction keeping the bike and rider attached to the wall due to the speed of the bike. Unfortunately this is an incorrect interpretation – remember centrifugal force is not a force - it is in fact a centripetal effect (a real force), the speed of the bike and friction keeping the rider there – the motorbike is trying to obey the laws of inertia and fly off through the walls of the cylinder – but the wooden wall acts as a barrier pushing back on the tyres of the bike - in other words, a centre seeking force acts on the tyres of the bike, while the bike, in effect, tries to drive through the boards at a tangent to the cylinder.

A person spinning a ball on a length of string offers a good insight to the forces at work on keeping the ball travelling in a circular path. Newton's first law of motion states that an object in motion stays in motion and that motion is in a straight path and not a circular path. Therefore as the ball is following a circular path then another force must be acting on the ball. This force is the string as it is trying to pull the ball back toward the person thus producing a centripetal effect. Please note that the string (in effect) imparts two forces on the ball, a force for tangential motion and another for the centripetal effect – if the string should snap (ending the centripetal effect) the ball will not fly away at right angles to the circle, but at a tangent to the circle obeying the first law of motion (inertia).

To reiterate we have said that a centrifugal force is not a real force. But a fictitious force and that a centripetal effect pulls an object toward the centre. Should this force stop working (e.g. the string breaks) then it is the object's inertia that takes over and sends the object travelling in a straight path. If you should doubt this then carry out a simple test by spinning a ball around you and letting go of the string. If centrifugal force was a real force, the ball would move straight away from you, at right angles to the circle, but it doesn't. Instead you will note that the ball follows its path of inertia and moves in a straight path that is tangent to the circular path.

Now consider an observer on the surface of the Earth - our planet appears to keep a constant distance from the Sun. It would seem to the observer, the Sun's gravity acting on Earth must be balanced by an equal and opposite force that keeps Earth at its constant distance. Thus, if gravity is trying to pull Earth into the Sun, some opposing force must be present to prevent that from happening. Thus who could blame the observer for calling this opposing balancing force a centrifugal force – an outward acting force?

But in reality, no such force exists and the observer is simply trying to make some kind of sense as to what is happening from his reference frame. If the observer knew the Earth was in accelerated motion (an orbiting planet is in fact a freely falling body) he would come to a different conclusion.

One of the pitfalls in understanding the mechanics of the ocean tides can be attributable to a misunderstanding and confusion in the use of the terms centripetal and centrifugal forces as we shall see later in the book.

Again I would respectfully suggest that a more accurate and less misleading term would be a CENTRIFUGAL EFFECT or perhaps drop the term altogether. Surely it is less confusing and more meaningful to say that it is a gravitational force and inertia that keeps the Moon in orbit about the Earth.

It is easily to become confused about 'centripetal and centrifugal forces', but actually there is no need to be, and you can clarify the situation quite simply for yourself - if an object is moving in a circle, there must be a force acting on it to make it turn, otherwise it would go in a straight line obeying Newton's first law of motion - so examine the situation and the object - carefully figuring out where the inward pushing or pulling force is coming from – that will be the centripetal effect – if the object or some part is flying outward it is not because of a force called centrifugal force, but because of the absence of a force – there is no force present for circular motion and the object then obeys Newton's first law of motion.

A good science teacher will tell you there is actually no such thing as centrifugal force. You can understand what's really happening by considering Isaac Newton's first law of motion, such that when (and to reiterate) a car begins to enter a bend, its natural tendency is to keep going in a straight line - and it will do so unless a force acts on it. When it follows the bend, it does so because there's a force constantly tugging it inward from its straight line course. What is considered as a centrifugal force is really the car's tendency (inertia) to follow a straight line.

Most of us are aware that astronauts and fighter pilots are tested and trained in what is known as large centrifuges to prepare them for extreme acceleration during lift-off from the surface of the Earth, or high acceleration in modern day fighter aircraft. Centrifuges simulate gravity – it is centripetal effect provided by the seat back pushing inward on the astronaut.

In the film 2001: A Space Odyssey (a 1968 epic science fiction film produced and directed by Stanley Kubrick) and inspired by a story by Arthur C. Clarke, we are introduced to a space station of circular and tubular design spinning slowly in Earth orbit. As seen in the film a large space station is slowly rotating in Earth orbit to produce artificial gravity whereby people are seen walking and jogging on the inner wall of the space station – the wall in effect becomes the floor. This is a realistic means to produce artificial gravity aboard a space station as it makes use of a centripetal effect to mimic the effects of gravity by pulling people toward the wall which is now the 'floor'.

Artificial gravity is the creation of an inertial force that mimics the effects of a gravitational force and should not be confused with the acceleration and subsequent G-force felt by an astronaut during take-off from the Earth's surface. For those who are not familiar with the definition of a G-force it stands for either the force of gravity on a particular celestial body, such as the Earth, or the force of acceleration anywhere in the Universe. It is measured in 'g' where 1 g is equal to the force of gravity at the Earth's surface and is 9.8 metres per second per second. As an example astronauts experience about 3 g's during take-off from the Earth's surface.

Fighter pilots can experience up to about 9 g vertically and wear 'G-suits' which helps push the blood away from their legs and towards the brain to stop them blacking out.

I will conclude this chapter with a couple of 'Thought Experiments' and for those not familiar with thought experiments they simply consider a hypothesis, theory, or principle for the purpose of thinking through its consequences. Einstein favoured thought experiments in determining and explaining many aspects of Relativity and I shall borrow his approach with the following:

Firstly, a simple thought experiment that will illustrate how the words centrifugal force belong in the world of Humpty Dumpty (Alice Through the Looking Glass) by quoting his words, "When I use a word, it means just what I choose it to mean - neither more nor less."

Thus imagine a large empty globe stationary in space whose walls have sufficient mass as to hold by gravitational attraction, two small bugs, one on the outside, and one on the inside at the equator of this imaginary sphere.

Now if we begin to rotate this sphere the bug on the inside will start to feel heavier, and as we gradually increase the speed, the bug will feel heavier and heavier as the G-force increases. If we keep increasing the speed there will come point when the bug will be crushed against the wall of the sphere – ugh!

The reason for this is simply down to Newton's first law of motion, or if you prefer to use fewer words, it is due to inertia. It is certainly not as a result of a 'new' force called a centrifugal force.

So what has happened to the bug on the surface of the sphere (at the equator) under the same conditions?

The bug on the surface will find the exact opposite is happening such that as the speed of the sphere increases the bug will feel lighter and lighter - as the speed increases the bug will eventually be thrown off the sphere into space at a tangent to the surface of the sphere. Again no 'new' force has appeared to snatch the bug off the sphere as the bug is also obeying Newton's first law of motion, or if you like, inertia.

Thus the reason the bug flew off into space was due to the fact that the centripetal effect was overcome, and not due to a pseudo-force called centrifugal force.

The Earth spins on its axis at about 1,674 km/hr (1,000 mph) at the equator, with an orbital speed of about 110,000 km/hr (67,000 mph). This means that if the Earth's gravity should suddenly cease, then we would not be thrown vertically upward, but tangentially from the surface of the Earth at about 1,674 km/hr into space – again not due to an imaginary force but because a real force has disappeared - and in this case gravity.

Earlier in the book we read how Isaac Newton compared the motion of the Moon to a cannon ball fired horizontally from a top of a high mountain and how it attained orbit. But what if the cannon ball was fired upwards towards space, then what would the speed of the cannon ball need to be to leave the Earth and travel into space? There is in fact a critical speed for a projectile to 'outrun' gravity and escape the Earth – this critical speed is called the *escape speed* or, if direction is involved, the *escape velocity*. From the surface of the Earth the escape velocity is 11.2 kilometres per second, and an object will move away from the Earth, slowing forever and approaching, but never reaching, zero speed.

Finally we will conclude this chapter with a final thought experiment as a summary and illustrating how misleading both the terms centripetal and centrifugal force are. I would claim the current terms are responsible for much of confusion surrounding objects that are forced to follow a circular path. Indeed centripetal and centrifugal forces, as mentioned earlier in this text, are not even proper forces in the sense of a real force, such as gravity or magnetism, but simply effects. So it is time the scientific world grasped the nettle and pronounced the terms should be more accurately called:

CENTRIPETAL AND CENTRIFUGAL EFFECTS

To qualify the above assertion, imagine a person and a solid wooden cube each with a mass of 80 kilogrammes on the surface of the Earth at the equator. Both the objects will have a mutual force of gravity of 784 newtons acting upon each of them due to the Earth, and they will be a considerable distance apart so the mutual attraction between the person and object may be ignored – the Earth's gravity will totally dominate. (See also appendix 2).

For this thought experiment we will imagine that initially the Earth is not rotating so the only force (ignoring such forces as wind) experienced by both objects is that of the Earth's gravity.

If we now imagine the Earth starting to spin on its axis then the situation changes as there are now effectively two forces beginning to act on the person and the cube - that of a downward pull of gravity plus a horizontal force imparted to the objects by the same gravity holding the objects to the surface of the now rotating planet.

Due to the Earth's rotation the gravitational force is attempting to move both objects in a straight line tangentially to the surface of the Earth, whilst at the same time holding them to the surface of the planet. A very good analogy is that of a conker on the end of a string being spun around a boy's body – the string is both imparting movement to the ball whilst stopping the ball fly away at a tangent to the circle it is making.

As the rotational speed of the Earth increases the person and the cube will become lighter and lighter until they are both flung off the Earth into space – but not upwards, but tangentially to the surface of the planet. The point at which gravity loses its grip on the objects is when the tangential force of the object exceeds that of gravity and in this case it is 784 newtons for each object.

Please note there has been no need to use the term centrifugal force simply because there is no such force. With regard to a stationary Earth the only force is the attractive force of gravity, but when the Earth starts to spin there is still the same gravitational force of attraction on objects stuck to its surface, but now motion has been imparted to the objects by the Earth's gravity – a centripetal effect.

If the Earth has been turning fast enough and should the Earth suddenly stop spinning, then both the objects will obey Newton's first law of motion and leave the Earth tangentially to its surface, flying off into space.

Having read this chapter I hope the reader will not be too dismayed with its repetitiveness, but it was felt necessary to drive home the difference between centripetal or centrifugal effects whilst exposing the fact of how centripetal and centrifugal effects are portrayed as forces when they are simply effects.

As mentioned earlier there has been a lot of nonsense written on how a centrifugal force plays a part in the rising of the tides on the far side of the Earth not facing the Moon, and it will be easily demonstrated that there is absolutely no need to consider centrifugal or centripetal effects at all in understanding the tides - the tides are simply the result of tidal gravity and free fall as the following chapters will show.

CHAPTER THREE

TIDAL GRAVITY

A lot of people may be forgiven for thinking the words tidal gravity and ocean tides actually stand for the same thing, when of course they do not. Although it is tidal gravity which is the cause of ocean tides it is vital to clarify the difference between the two.

To appreciate what is meant by ocean tides one has only to simply stand on a beach with a reasonable tidal range watching the ebb and flow of the tide, and being cut-off by a high tide will certainly bring the message home; but the term tidal gravity needs a more detailed qualification to its full meaning. The consideration of certain celestial bodies such as comets, meteors, and especially a Black Hole, will clearly show the meaning of tidal gravity. Thus we will start this chapter by considering a number of famous comets and meteors.

COMETS AND METEORS

Arguably the most famous comet is that of Halley's Comet. It appeared early in 1066 AD before the Battle of Hastings. It is shown on the famous Bayeux Tapestry, which documents the Battle of Hastings, which saw William the Conqueror and the Normans defeat the Saxons led by Harold Godwinson.

Edmond Halley calculated the orbit of Halley's Comet in 1705, but it was sadly unfortunate that he died before it appeared in 1758. The comet is about 15 kilometres long and takes approximately 75 years to orbit around the Sun and is known as short period comet – the comet is said to have originated from the Oort Cloud of the Solar

System - short period comets complete their orbits in less than 200 years.

For those not familiar with astronomy, the Oort Cloud is a region in outer space that contains large quantities of ice such as comets, being located in the outermost regions of the Solar System; past the Kuiper Belt.

The Kuiper Belt is a circumstellar disc in the outer Solar System, beyond the Asteroid Belt, extending from the orbit of Neptune (at 30 AU) to approximately 50 AU from the Sun, encompassing Pluto. It is similar to the Asteroid Belt, but is far larger.

The Astronomical Unit (AU) is a unit of astronomical measurement and represents the mean distance between the Earth and the Sun. An AU is approximately 93 million miles (150 million kilometres), and is approximately 8 light-minutes away from us – this means it takes about 8 minutes for the Sun's light to reach us on Earth – so should the Sun mysteriously cease to exist, whilst reading these words, you will not know, dear reader, until 8 minutes have elapsed.

The Asteroid Belt is a doughnut-shaped belt located between the orbits of Mars and Jupiter and is occupied by numerous irregularly shaped bodies called asteroids or minor planets. Occasionally asteroids can be perturbed from their orbit – those that pass close to the Earth (and can be a threat) and are called Near-Earth Objects (NEOs).

Halley's Comet was last seen in 1986, when it was studied by spacecraft and will not return until 2061.

The well known American writer Mark Twain was born during a Halley's Comet appearance in 1835. He predicted he would die when it next appeared and actually died the year after the next appearance that happened, in 1910.

Comets are made up of a mixture of frozen gases and solid materials being irregular in shape. Halley's Comet consists of ammonia, sodium, carbon monoxide, water and iron – some describe comets as being akin to dirty snowballs.

The first record of Halley's Comet was found in the Chinese chronicle 'Records of the Grand Historian or Shiji' that describes a comet as moving toward the north from the east.

GREAT COMETS

The Great Comet of 1680: Discovered on November 14th, 1680, by a German astronomer called Gottfried Kirch and has the distinction of being the first comet discovered by telescope – it was one of the brightest comets of the 17th Century being visible during daylight hours and had a particularly long tail.

The Great Comet of 1744: First sighted on November 29th, 1743, as a dim object, but brightened rapidly as it approached the Sun. By February the comet rivalled the star Sirius in brightness and displayed a curved tail 15 degrees in length – and by February the comet was as bright as Venus and now displayed two tails – toward the end of February was reported to be visible in the daytime, During March the comet appeared in the morning sky, and was observed with six brilliant tails that looked like a Japanese hand fan.

The Great Comet of 1811: Discovered on March 25th, 1811, and was visible to the naked eye for around 260 days, a record it held until the appearance of Comet Hale–Bopp in 1997. During October, 1811, when at its brightest, it displayed an easily visible and exceptionally large coma. The year 1811 turned out to be particularly fine for wine production, with wine merchants selling "Comet Wine"- and at high prices for many years afterwards.

The Great Comet of 1843: This comet appeared in the sky as an elongated white cloud, with a brilliant head, whereby passengers on a ship off the Cape of Good Hope described the comet as being like a short dagger-like object that closely followed the Sun toward the western horizon. The comet had an extremely long tail measuring

320 million kilometres (200 million miles) which is greater than the distance between Mars and the Sun.

Great September Comet of 1882: Spotted by Italian sailors on September 1st, 1882, in the Southern Hemisphere. It became visible in daylight and is claimed to be the brightest comet ever seen – observers in Spain described the comet as a blazing star near the Sun. Modern comet historians consider it as a Super Comet and in a league of its own when discussing great comets.

Great January Comet of 1910: First spotted in South Africa on January 13th, 1910. Visible during the day being brighter than the planet Venus and could be seen as an amazing object in the evening sky.

The Great Comet Skjellerup-Maristanny, 1927: First seen in early December, 1927, and became visible during the day later in December – had an impressively long tail.

The Great Comet Ikeya-Seki, 1965: The brightest comet of the 20th Century. In Japan the comet was claimed to be about ten times brighter than a full Moon.

The Great Comet West, 1976: In the Northern Hemisphere this comet became a beautiful object in the morning sky during early March, 1976. The comet was named after the Danish astronomer Richard West, who discovered it in November, 1975.

The Great Comet McNaught, 2007: Discovered by Australian astronomer Robert McNaught and became a brilliant object during January, 2007. Unfortunately for Northern Hemisphere observers the best views of the comet were mainly from south of the equator where it developed a huge fan-shaped tail. Observers during the day in Hawaii claimed the comet appeared much brighter than Venus.

The Tunguska Event, 1908: Considered not a comet, but a meteor. On the morning of 30th June, 1908, a huge explosion occurred in the skies near the Stony Tunguska River in Russia. Although classified as an impact event (although no impact crater has been found) it is generally accepted that a meteor exploded and disintegrated about between 5 and 10 kilometres (3 to 6 miles) above the ground. In doing so it is estimated that 2,000 square kilometres (770 square miles) of forest was flattened – it is estimated that something in the region of 80 million trees were knocked down.

Luckily the area is sparsely populated and no known human casualties were reported. It should be noted that the Tunguska Event is the largest impact in recorded history and different studies have offered different estimates of the objects size ranging from 60 to 190 metres (200 to 620 feet) depending if indeed the object was a loosely packed comet or a denser meteor.

For those not familiar with the terms a meteor is an asteroid or other celestial object that burns and vaporises when entering the Earth's atmosphere; meteors are commonly known as 'shooting stars'. But if a meteor survives the journey through the atmosphere and lands or impacts the surface, it is known as a meteorite – meteorites are usually categorised as iron or stony.

So what causes a meteor to break up in the atmosphere?

Celestial particles about the size of a grain of sand on hitting the Earth's atmosphere will burn up due to their high speed and the friction afforded by atmospheric gasses – we see these at night as shooting stars. As mentioned above, relatively small objects such as small rocks comprised of iron or stone, will survive intact in their passage through the atmosphere and impact with the ground. Larger objects, depending on speed, size and composition will break up a few kilometres above the Earth's surface.

As mentioned earlier in this chapter comets can be regarded as similar to a giant snowball and can measure from 100 metres to more than 40 kilometres across, being composed of a mixture of rock, dust, ice and frozen gasses such as carbon dioxide, methane, ammonia and carbon monoxide. Because of their make-up comets are held together relatively loosely by their mass and gravity, whereas meteors being mostly composed of rock and iron and are much tighter bound together. Obviously this has the effect of comet's breaking up more easily in a strong gravity field than meteors – the tidal force of a large mass such as the planet Jupiter stretching it apart will be greater than the gravity that holds the comet together.

Comets, or loosely packed meteors, when fatally attracted toward a very large body, such as a planet and its strong gravitational field will meet their nemesis.

Such bodies are pulled apart due to the pulling and stretching as a result of the difference in gravity across the body – as a comet or meteor plummets towards the planet the force of gravity will be greater at the part of the object nearer the planet than at the part furthest from the planet – creating a difference in forces across the object causing the comet or meteor to breakup. So in conjunction with atmospheric friction this is deemed the cause of the Tunguska object to explode above the Tunguska forest.

Comet Shoemaker-Levy 9: Perhaps a better example of the tidal gravity effect would be that of the comet Shoemaker-Levy 9 (SL9) which broke apart before impacting with the giant planet Jupiter. There was extensive world-wide coverage being closely observed by astronomers as the first sighting of a collision of Solar System celestial objects. The comet came too close to the massive planet Jupiter back in July, 1992. Comets are very fragile objects, and SL9, for example, started breaking up when the powerful forces of Jupiter's gravity began pulling at it - exerting what is called a 'tidal force', pulling more strongly at the side of the comet closest to the planet. The uneven pull was just too much for the tiny comet and its internal forces (gravity) could no longer hold it together, and thus the comet fragmented.

It was the astronomers Eugene and Carolyn Shoemaker with David Levy that discovered the unusual comet in the vicinity of Jupiter during March, 1993. The comet consisted of about a dozen comet nuclei lined up like glowing pearls on a string – as the nuclei spread further apart a total of 21 fragments were seen. Investigation of their common orbit revealed that the original and un-fragmented comet had been moving about the Sun and then had been captured into orbit around the giant planet Jupiter in about 1929. In passing very close to the planet in July, 1992, tidal forces from the giant planet's gravity broke the original comet nucleus, about 1.6 kilometre (1 mile) in diameter, into 21 pieces.

The fragmented comet adopted a very eccentric two year orbit around Jupiter. Then gravitational perturbations by the Sun changed the orbit whereby the comet's fragments then passed even closer to Jupiter causing the 21 nuclei to impact Jupiter in July, 1994 at a velocity of 221,000 kilometres per hour (137,000 mph). The event was observed from telescopes worldwide, the Hubble Space telescope, other orbiting instruments and the Galileo spacecraft which was on its way to Jupiter.

The Chelyabinsk Meteor, 2013: This near-Earth asteroid entered the Earth's atmosphere over Russia on 15th February, 2013 with a speed of about 64,000 kilometres per hour (40,000 mph) and quickly became a brilliant meteor with a light brighter than the Sun – some witnesses claimed they could feel the heat from the fireball. The object entered the atmosphere at a shallow angle and exploded at a height of about 29 kilometres (18 miles) over Chelyabinsk Oblast.

The meteor is the largest known object to have entered the Earth's atmosphere since the Tunguska event in 1908 and although it resulted in a large number of injuries (mainly from broken glass from windows shattering) no fatalities were reported.

The explosion of the Chelyabinsk meteor is another good example of what happens to an object entering the atmosphere and gravity field of a planet at high speed, where the friction of the atmospheric gasses causes the object to heat up, and coupled with tidal gravity will cause the object to disintegrate.

We have digressed into the realms of comets, meteors and how objects can be affected by a planet's atmosphere and gravitational attraction, but I hope it has been an interesting and useful exercise.

I find it truly enigmatic that so many sources invoke a centrifugal force in an attempt to explain the tidal bulge on the far side of the Earth away from the Moon? I can only guess it is due to the confusion and misconception between centrifugal and centripetal forces. Indeed we have seen that centrifugal is not a force in the sense of the four main forces, such as gravity, but a fictitious force and I make no apology for the reiteration in my efforts at pressing the 'truth' home.

Centripetal force is a generic name for any force that keeps an object moving with a uniform speed along a circular path. The gravitational pull of the Earth's gravity on the Moon, or that of a piece of string connected to a ball being whirled around your head, are good examples.

But recognise that in whirling a ball about our head that there is not a pull on the string directly towards us, but a tangential tug with the string imparting motion to the ball, whilst at the same time the string itself stops (centripetal force) the ball flying away tangentially.

Note that if we laid the ball on the ground and pulled the ball directly towards us with the string, the ball would come towards us in a straight line, as only one force (overcoming gravity and neglecting friction) acts on the ball – it is purely a direct force as we pull on the string directly towards us.

In mentioning tidal gravity it is easy to assume we are talking about coastal tides, but tidal gravity encompasses a lot more than the tides of the ocean and it is very important to fully understand how tidal gravity affects objects in motion.

Direct gravitational attraction works as an attractive force such as keeping us, the oceans and atmospheric gasses attached to the Earth – without gravity the Earth would soon lose its atmosphere. Taking a brick to the top of a high building then releasing it to fall to the ground is a clear demonstration to the effects of direct gravity over a short distance – indeed dropping a brick on your foot will serve as an unforgettable lesson.

Over relatively long distances gravity has a different effect on moving objects to the extent it can pull them apart. The comet Shoemaker-Levy 9 as mentioned earlier is a classic example, the comet being broken up by the gravitational field of the giant planet Jupiter.

The breaking apart of celestial bodies arises because the gravitational field exerted on one body by another is not constant across its parts: the nearest side is attracted more strongly than the farthest side. It is this difference that causes a body to get stretched. Thus, the tidal force is also known as the differential force, as well as a secondary effect of the gravitational field.

In celestial mechanics there is a limit (point) in which a celestial body, held together by its own gravity, will disintegrate due the influence of the gravitational tidal forces of a second body exceeding the gravity (gravitational self-attraction) of the first body. This limit is known as the Roche limit.

The breaking up of comet Shoemaker-Levy by the strong gravitational force of the giant planet Jupiter is child's play when compared to the tidal forces of a Black Hole, which are among the strangest things in the known Universe.

A Black Hole is a region of space with gravity so strong that nothing, including light, can escape – around a Black Hole there is a point of no return called the Event Horizon – the boundary at which the gravitational pull of a massive object becomes so great as to make escape impossible. Even light emitted from inside the Event Horizon can never reach an outside observer – all light that hits a Black Hole is absorbed, it reflects nothing and that is why Black Holes are black as all light cannot escape from them. It is thought that Black Holes are to be found at the centre of many galaxies including our own, the Milky Way.

Any object unfortunate to experience falling into a Black Hole will be exposed to different experiences; but if you should be unlucky enough to find yourself falling, feet first, into a relatively small Black Hole you will be stretched like a piece of spaghetti due to the nearest side being attracted very much greater than the farthest side – as you fall toward the Black Hole you will accelerate faster and faster due to its enormous gravity – your feet feel a much stronger gravitational pull than your head – the result is your body being stretched apart - indeed torn apart before you even reach the Event Horizon.

The situation is different for a super-massive Black Hole where cosmologists say your body will remain intact until you pass the Event Horizon and then squashed into a single point of infinite density – you will then be part of the Black Hole.

Black Holes truly illustrate how differential gravity commonly known as tidal gravity work.

Tidal gravity also produces tidal heating in solid bodies with its pulling and stretching effects. Jupiter' moon Io is a good example as it orbits the giant planet's gravitational field. The moon is pulled and stretched producing dramatic volcanic effects as depicted in pictures sent back from the NASA Galileo spacecraft in close encounters in the 1990s and early 2000s.

Tidal forces are also responsible for monthly moonquakes on our Moon as a result of the Earth's gravity – therefore it is true to say that tidal gravity can cause seismic events.

Now if we consider a small elastic sphere falling in a gravitational field of a large body, the effect of a tidal force is to distort the shape of the body without any change in volume - the sphere takes on an elliptical shape with two bulges, pointing in and away from the source of the gravitational field, as we shall see in the next chapter.

We will end this chapter by considering three *thought experiments* such that in the first experiment imagine a planet and moon similar in size to our own planet and moon. Both being separated by the same distance apart as our Moon and the Earth, but in this case the planet is completely covered in an ocean a thousand feet deep, and both bodies are not rotating nor orbiting about each other in space, and being 'magically' held apart.

If we were to ask ourselves, if the planet will experience any tides (will there be a tidal bulge)? The answer to the question is a resounding no as the gravity of the planet will certainly dominate holding the oceans at the same level all around the planet. The planet's attendant moon has a much lower mass coupled with the fact that it much more distant from the planet's centre of gravity than the planet's oceans. Thus the inverse square law will greatly diminish the effect of the moon's gravity on the oceans to the extent that it will have a negligible effect, and the planet's gravitational force of attraction will dominate.

Now consider a second *thought experiment* where the same two bodies are in space but this time the planet is rotating on its axis, whilst the moon does not rotate on its axis. Again we ask the same question relating to tides where again the answer is there will not be a tidal bulge - even considering the miniscule so-called centrifugal force generated by the rotation of the planet being of the same magnitude as the Earth at about 1600 kilometres per hour at the equator.

In the third thought experiment the moon is now orbiting around the stationary planet but again there will be no tidal bulge or indeed any centrifugal effect – the planet's far greater gravitational force will hold the oceans to its surface.

For those who wish a mathematical qualification to the above *thought experiments* then there are a number of examples in the appendices of this book.

How the tides come about on a planet such as the Earth will now be explained in the next chapter.

CHAPTER FOUR

OCEAN TIDES

Having reached this part of the book we know that a pretend force called centrifugal force plays no part in the cause of the ocean tides – common sense demands 'how can it' when it is a fictitious force.

So we will now proceed and see how the tides are produced on our planet.

In the previous chapter we imagined a planet and moon similar in size and distance apart as the Earth and our Moon – but in this case both bodies were not moving and were motionless in space. In this imaginary scenario there would be no so-called centrifugal force, as the Earth is not spinning, nor for that matter would there be any centripetal force. Additionally there would be the 'absence' of free fall as the two bodies are not orbiting about their centre of gravity (barycentre). The question was posed of what will happen to the oceans on the planet under these circumstances – and the simple answer was that there would not be any tides due to the absence of motion coupled with the gravity of the planet dominating the oceans and holding the waters down - not forgetting the inverse square law in relation to the distance of its moon diminishing its gravitational effect on the oceans.

Now regarding our own planet, the Earth, a number of sources claim that a so-called centrifugal force is instrumental in raising the tides on the far side of the Earth furthest from the Moon, but as we have seen this is ridiculous. The nonsense overlooks the fact that the Earth, being spheroid, centrifugal force would act equally around the equator of our planet in the same context as gravity being the same around the equator of our planet. No doubt Lewis Carroll's Alice would have asked Humpty Dumpty, "So where is the logic and sense in claiming that a pseudo-force actually plays a part in raising the tides."

It would also appear the 'centrifugal disciples' have truly overlooked the centripetal force of the Earth. For how can a relatively weak so-called centrifugal force exceed the gravity of the Earth holding the mass of the oceans to the surface of the Earth?

Ocean tides have nothing to do with purely a direct gravitational attraction from the Moon, and it would also appear the 'centrifugal disciples' have also overlooked the inverse square law relating to gravity. In explaining the mechanism behind the tides there is a much more logical and common sense approach, and there is absolutely no need to use the terms centrifugal or centripetal force. In adopting a different and more sensible approach lends itself to a much easier and understandable explanation that does not fall into the traps of misconception and needless complication.

The answer is quite simple and our tides are due to tidal gravity

Although to be more exact:

The ocean tides are the result of tidal gravity due to the Earth falling toward the Moon and to a lesser extent of the Earth and Moon system falling toward the Sun.

But if the Earth is falling toward the Moon what is stopping the inevitable collision between the Earth and the Moon – indeed, at first sight these words would seem preposterous for if the Earth is falling toward the Moon, why has the Earth and Moon not collided eons ago – and why has the Earth and Moon system not collided with the Sun? Those unfamiliar with the forces behind the ocean tides these will seem strange words and possibly protest that the Earth does not fall toward the Moon, neither does the Earth and Moon fall toward the Sun, claiming it is nonsense!

Thus we appear to have an enigma.

As mentioned earlier in this book most people when asked how the ocean tides are raised would offer that it is mainly because of the pull of the Moon and to a lesser extent the pull of the Sun, implying that it is the effect of the direct gravitational attraction of these celestial bodies.

In other words they are saying that on the side of the Earth facing the Moon it is the Moon's gravity that is pulling directly on the oceans and drawing them upward in the direction of the Moon. Now this has to be nonsense as the Earth will attract a person to its surface far greater than the Moon - otherwise we would all be very much lighter in weight under a full Moon – methinks a touch of lunacy!

If the tides were a consequence of purely the direct attraction of the gravitational pull of the Moon, then it could also be argued that the oceans would pile up on the side of the Earth nearest the Moon and there would not be an appreciable ocean bulge on the side of the Earth furthest from the Moon; indeed, ocean water on the opposite side of the Earth would surely flow to replenish water drained from the Earth's surface at right angles to the Moon. Additionally when the Sun, Moon and Earth are in direct alignment with the Sun and Moon, on the same side of the Earth, then the combination of both the Sun and the Moon's gravitational pull would exacerbate the situation.

But we know there are other influences at work as the Moon orbits the Earth, and Earth with its Moon orbits the Sun; **it is these motions that are the key.**

So if the ocean bulge is not as a consequence of the direct gravitational pull of the Moon and Sun, then how do these orbital motions contribute to the tides we experience on Earth; what forces are at work to cause these ocean tides as we know them?

With our understanding now of barycentre, free fall et cetera we shall now explore this phenomenon.

The gravitational forces of both the Moon, and to a lesser degree the Sun, are obviously involved in the mechanics of the ocean tides, but not in the way most people perceive these forces to operate. Although the Sun has the greater mass – hence – the greater gravitational force – it is the Moon that has the most marked effect upon the ocean tides due to its closer proximity. The effect of the gravitational force of one body upon another is dependent upon the inverse-square law (Isaac Newton).

Thus the Sun being some 400 times further from the Earth than is the Moon will have its effective gravitational force reduced much more substantially - nevertheless it does have some effect in its own right upon the oceans of the world. The oceans are also much nearer to the centre of the Earth than the centre of the Moon.

Before proceeding further it should be noted that there are land and atmospheric tides, but these occur on a very much smaller scale - the probability of earthquakes and similar activity, is slightly higher when the planet is experiencing 'Spring Tides' such as at new or full Moon. It should be noted the atmospheric tides are not detected by human senses as the air has low mass - these tides are not as pronounced as the land tides, indeed they are very small.

It is important to keep in mind what is happening to mass when it is in a state of Free Fall; remember that astronauts do not feel the pull of the Earth's gravity when orbiting the Earth in their space craft. Their weightlessness is not due to the reduction in the Earth's gravitational force, but due to the fact that the downward acceleration of their space craft exactly cancels the pull of the Earth's gravity – the astronauts are in Free Fall. Now it is also important to keep in mind that both the Earth and the Moon are in Free Fall around each other, or more precisely around their common centre (barycentre) of mass.

This means that similar to the case of the astronauts in Free Fall anything on the surface of the Earth or Moon will not experience the direct gravitational pull of each other. We also know the immensity of the Sun's gravity when compared to the Earth and the Moon. Indeed, it is this gravity that keeps the Earth in orbit around the Sun - but your weight is not affected when the Sun is overhead - nor would your respective weight be affected by the Sun being overhead on Mercury and as we know Mercury is the closest planet to the Sun!

The ocean tides occur due to the 'difference' in the way the Moon's gravity pulls on 'different' parts of the Earth as a result of the Earth falling toward the Moon; this difference in the Moon's gravity causes a stretching and squeezing of the oceans. It is this stretching and squeezing that causes the Earth's tides. As we have already said the Earth and the Moon are in free fall around each other, or to be more precise, around their common centre (barycentre) of mass. This means that the oceans of the Earth are in effect falling toward the Moon.

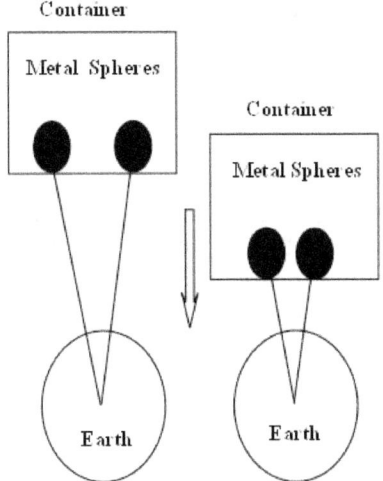

The paths of the two objects falling toward the centre of the Earth will converge and meet at the centre of the Earth

Imagine a large container in the shape of a box about five thousand kilometres above the Earth's surface with two solid metal spherical objects inside placed on the floor – that is, the inside surface nearest the Earth's surface.

The large container with the two spherical objects is allowed to fall and as such will plummet towards the Earth's surface under the influence of gravity. It is important to remember that gravity operates from the geometric centre of the Earth and as such the gravitational field will have a radial configuration. Thus any two falling objects will converge and (theoretically) meet at the centre of the Earth – looking inside the box the two metal spheres will be seen to move toward each other.

Now we know from Newton that if two such spherical balls were arranged adjacent to each other and about a metre apart in deep space with no other mass (or gravitational field) close by to influence the spheres, then the two balls would be attracted and move toward one another till they met. If both spheres were of identical mass they would move together at the same rate, as they would be exerting the same force on each other.

Returning to our falling container with the two objects we can safely ignore the effect of their mutual gravity, as the Earth's gravity is so enormously much greater than that of the two spheres. Thus with the two objects falling toward the geometric centre of the Earth it means their paths will converge and as such they will move together, regardless of any mutual attraction.

Now that we have seen how two objects move together when in free fall, let us examine the case for four such spheres.

Imagine we now have four solid metallic and spherical objects falling toward the Earth. The objects are arranged to form a diamond shape with one point of the diamond (one sphere) nearest the Earth and leading the way down and the opposite point (top sphere) coming last.

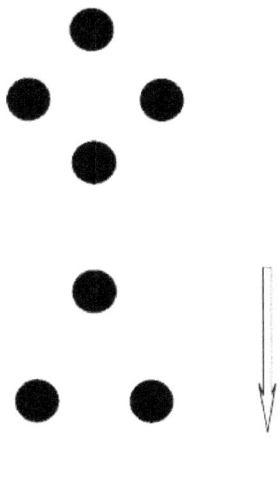

Four solid metal spheres fall toward the Earth in free fall. The differences in the gravitational pull of the Earth on each of them causes them to fall differently. The sphere nearest the Earth falls more rapidly than the others and gets ahead. The sphere farthest from the Earth falls less rapidly and lags behind.

The outside pair of spheres beside falling less rapidly than the sphere closest to the Earth also move together as shown in the diagram to the left.

All the four spheres are in free fall. The highest sphere is at the greatest distance from the Earth and as gravity decreases with distance, so the attraction between this highest object and the Earth is less than the attraction between its three companions and the Earth. Thus it lags further and further behind the others as they fall. The lowest sphere has the greatest attraction, as it is closest to the Earth and thus travels the fastest increasing its lead as the objects fall.

The other two spheres fall at the same rate, but their paths converge. The ultimate result is that the diamond configuration of the four spheres becomes distorted and it is the difference in the strength of gravity from place to place that causes the distortion.

Now suppose we exchange the four metal spheres for one sphere made of soft and pliable plastic and allow that to fall under the influence of gravity.

Thus the same forces will act upon the sphere of plastic as in the previous case of the four metal spheres - as the plastic sphere continues to fall the effects of squeezing and stretching the plastic will cause it to become more ovoid in shape. This vertical stretch and lateral squeeze is due to gravitational forces known as tidal gravity.

From what we have learnt from the above we can now go ahead in understanding the mechanism of the ocean tides.

The Moon and the Earth are in free fall orbit and nothing on the surface of the Moon or the Earth can feel the direct gravity of the other body. However, as happened in our thought experiment, the Earth, the Moon and things on the surface of them can be affected by the 'difference' in the strength of the gravitational field from place to place and the 'difference' that makes in the way they fall.

The result being that the waters on the side of the Earth nearest the Moon bulge out moonward, making a high tide. The opposite side of the Earth effectively gets left behind a little, as in the case of the falling metal spheres, making a second high tide. In between there are low tides due to the squeezing effect and the 'squashed' waters contribute to the ocean bulges.

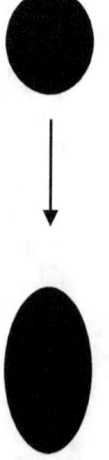

A sphere of soft plasticine free falling toward the Earth would have tidal forces acting upon it. This would result in the squeezing and stretching of the plasticine causing it to distort and become more ovoid.

In explaining the mechanism of the ocean tides we have ignored the effect of the Sun's gravitational pull for although it does have an influence it is of a lesser nature due to its distance in comparison to the proximity of the Moon.

Although the Sun's mutual gravity is about 180 times stronger than the Moon's mutual gravity, solar tides are not as big as lunar tides. This is because of the difference between the Sun's gravity on the side of the Earth nearest the Sun and the side of the Earth furthest from the Sun is small. The Sun is very much further away from the Earth than the Moon and the distance from one side of the Earth to the other is so small in comparison to the distance of the Earth from the Sun that it makes very little difference in the effect imposed by the Sun.

To summarise our study of the ocean tides so far, we have stated that the bulge on the side of the Earth furthest from the Moon appears to be somewhat enigmatic when related to purely a direct gravitational force, as apart from any inertial effect one would expect most of the oceans to be pulled toward and bulge out on the surface of the Earth nearest to the Moon. If the oceans of the Earth's were subjected to the direct effect of the pull of the Moon then, theoretically, it could be argued that this would indeed be the result; the oceans would tend to pile up on the side of the Earth facing and nearest to the Moon. But we have seen this is not the case as the fundamental mechanism behind the ocean tides is due to the phenomenon known as tidal gravity.

Other Factors Contributing to the Ocean Tides

As the land masses and the oceans, are not uniform there are many exceptions to the basic theory - there are negligible tides in the Baltic and the Mediterranean; being almost completely land locked there is no effective movement of water – as the water tends to move (under the effect lunar and solar gravity) there is no water to flow into the resultant hollows and the back pressure prevents the forward movement - this of course particularly applies to lakes and totally inland seas. Due to its vast mass the Pacific Ocean does not follow the basic theory and in some parts has only one tidal cycle per day.

The difference between high and low tide can be considerable at places that are quite close together, as an example, on the French coast in Mont St Michel Bay the tidal range is approximately 14 metres whilst at Cherbourg, a hundred kilometres up the coast, it is only 6.6 metres. There are some even more startling differences in other parts of the World. In the Bay of Fundy (Canada) the maximum range is 19.69 metres, whilst at Portishead on the Bristol Channel it is 15.75 metres. At the other end of the scale in the mid-Pacific the tidal range is very low at just under 2 metres in the Marquesas. In the Mediterranean it is even lower and on the shores of the Adriatic it is only 1.3 metres.

There are also periodic variations in the interplay of the two prime gravitational forces that affect the tidal heights caused by the elliptical orbit of the Earth around the Sun and that of the Moon around the Earth.

The study and understanding of ocean movements and the theory of tides is a very complex subject. The variation of the seashores, channels, estuaries, beach steepness, ocean currents and size of the ocean all play their part. As we have seen above there is a very marked difference in tides of the Mediterranean and that of Mont St Michel Bay, Northern France, Therefore the ultimate and actual behaviour of the tides lies not in the province of astronomy but in that of hydrography and physical geography.

Spring Tides

The highest tides, known as Spring Tides, occur around the time of a New and Full Moon. That is when the Sun, Moon and Earth are in direct alignment.

Spring Tides result in higher-than-average high tides and lower-than-average low tides. A consequence of the elliptical nature of the orbits of the Earth and the Moon is that the distance between the Sun, Earth and Moon vary. This means that all Spring Tides are not equally high. Indeed, the distance between the Earth and the Moon varies by about 10 percent, which results in a 30 percent difference in the Moon's effect in raising tides.

Neap Tides

The Sun and Moon's tidal pull are virtually at right angles during the first and last quarter of the Moon. As such the ocean tides have their lowest amplitude.

These tides are known as Neap Tides.

Therefore the high tides are lower than average and the low tides are not as low as the average low tides. In summary, the reason behind the ocean tides can be stated as:

The result of tidal gravity due to the Earth falling toward the Moon, and to a lesser extent, the Earth and Moon system, falling toward the Sun.

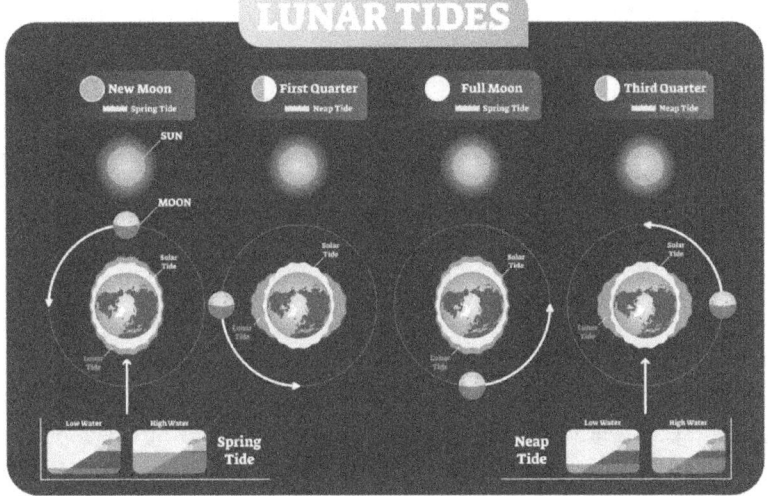

This being dependent on:

❖ The mass (gravity) of the Moon.

❖ The mass (gravity) of the Sun.

❖ Rotation of the Earth on its axis.

❖ Position of the Earth, Moon and Sun with respect to one another.

❖ Varying distance between the Earth and the Moon.

❖ Varying distance between the Earth and the Sun.

❖ Inclination of the Moon's orbit.

❖ Variation in the shape of coastlines and relief of ocean basins.

There are generally two high tides and two low tides every 24 hours due mainly to the Moon's gravitational effect and the motion of the Moon and Earth.

Having dealt with the basic mechanisms of ocean tides it is deemed outside the scope of this book to address the subject of terrestrial tides any further. The understanding of ocean movements is a very complex subject. Therefore those wishing to pursue the matter further should be aware there are many books encompassing hydrography and physical geography on the market to adequately satisfy this need.

Cherishing the Planet

Next time you are on a beach remember that any rubbish left behind on the sands or pebbles will eventually be washed out to sea with the tides. The planet is abused in many ways and the oceans due to tides and currents are polluted from pole to pole, with plastic and other waste. One of the consequences of all this neglect being the injury and death to many marine creatures – many are trapped by, or die attempting to eat this obnoxious waste.

Polluting the oceans is totally irresponsible and bad enough, but in compounding this felony, why should Government allow the industrialisation of our beautiful and irreplaceable British countryside with unpredictable and unreliable wind farms and solar parks – the only sure thing you can predict about the Sun as an energy source is that it does not shine at night. Attempting to generate large scale and reliable electricity from wind or sun in the British Isles is doomed to failure. It is madness that we pay wind farms when they are not even producing electricity due to potentially damaging high winds. Pity the poor consumer in the middle of winter when there is no wind or sunlight.

It is incomprehensible that in the early part of the 21st Century the UK is not producing significant amounts of clean electricity from the tides and ocean currents – do we not live on an island! The Bristol Channel has the second highest tidal range on the planet and is capable of producing a significant amount of UK electrical energy, then there are the tidal surges through the Menai Straits and between Ramsey Island and the mainland – and that is just a sample of the tidal potential around Wales – what about the rest of the British Isles - surely a case of not being able to see the wood for the trees - or perhaps more meaningfully, not being able to see the beach for the seaweed?

Indeed, it is totally unforgiveable that Westminster will not support the Swansea Bay Tidal Lagoon Project as apart from producing clean and reliable electrical energy and creating much needed employment, it will act as a great tourist attraction helping the local economy, in the same way as the Dinorwig Pumped Electricity Station, Llanberis, North Wales has demonstrated. The station is known as Snowdonia's 'Electric Mountain Centre' which houses shops, a café, art displays and a children's soft-play area; and is the starting point for tours of Dinorwig Power Station. Think and consider the fantastic potential of the Swansea Bay Lagoon Project – the myopic, unimaginative, technological, engineering, and business challenged Ministers at Westminster have a lot to answer for – but then why is the Welsh Assembly and Welsh Office not fighting *tooth and nail* for this project. Wales and indeed the UK have the potential to become a world leader in tidal energy, but where is the leadership - perhaps it has gone out with the tide?

Well we have come to the end of the book dear reader and I hope that apart from having a clear insight to the so-called centrifugal and centripetal forces, you are now fully conversant to the nature of the tides – but most importantly you can now appreciate the madness of not exploiting all this tidal energy for the common good – electrical energy from the tides is both clean and reliable, being worlds apart from dangerous and dirty nuclear power stations – remember, not one nuclear power station in the UK has yet to be totally and safely decommissioned.

Appendix 1

Useful Data

Equatorial radius of the Earth = 6.38 x 10^6 m.
Equatorial radius of the Moon = 1.74 x 10^6 m.
Equatorial radius of the Sun = 6.96 x 10^8 m.

Mass of the Earth = 5.98 x 10^{24} kg.
Mass of the Moon = 7.36 x 10^{22} kg.
Mass of the Sun = 1.99 x 10^{30} kg.

Average Earth-Moon distance = 3.84 x 10^8 m.
Average Earth-Sun distance = 1.50 x 10^{11} m.

Earths equatorial velocity = 1,675 km/h, 465 m/s (about 1,040 mph).
Earth's escape speed (velocity) = 11.2 km/s.
Earth's orbital speed = 110,000 km/h, (67,000 mph).

G = Universal gravitational constant (6.67 x 10^{-11} N-m^2/kg^2).

Acceleration due to gravity at the surface of the Earth = 9.80 m/s^2

Centripetal acceleration at the equator = 9.80 m/s^2.
Centrifugal acceleration at the equator = 0.034 m/s^2.

Escape Velocity of Earth = 11.2 km/s, or 11,184 m/s (7 miles/second, or 25,000 miles/hour).

1 kilogramme = 2.2 lbs.
1 kilogramme-force = 9.80665 newtons.

The unit of force is the newton (N) where gravity exerts a force of 9.8 N on each kilogramme of mass.

1 newton is approximately 0.225 lbs or 0.102 kilogrammes.

Altitude of International Space Station (ISS) is approximately 400 kilometres (248 miles).

Velocity of ISS is approximately 27,500 Km/h, or 7.8 Km/s (17,600 mph, or 5 mile/second).

The ISS orbits the earth about once every 90 minutes.

Escape velocity from the Earth = 11.3 kilometres (7 miles) per second.

Speed: The motion of an object over a certain distance in a given time and is a measure of how something is moving. It is measured in terms of a unit distance divided by a unit of time. Examples are 20 kilometres per hour or 20 miles per hour.

Velocity: This is a component of both speed and direction such as travelling 20 kilometres an hour in a northerly direction.

Acceleration: Occurs when there is a change of velocity – that is a change of speed or direction, or a change simultaneously of both speed and direction.

$F = G \, m_e m_o / d^2$
$F = ma$
$F = m \, v^2 / r$
$a = v^2 / r$
$W = mg$

Escape Velocity of Earth $(v_e) = \sqrt{2Gm/r}$

Appendix 2

Newton's Universal Law of Gravitation

Newton's law of Universal Gravitation states that every mass in the Universe attracts every other mass with a force that for two masses is directly proportional to the product of their masses and inversely proportional to the square of the distance separating them. When a constant known as the universal gravitational constant (G) is introduced we can describe Newton's law of gravity in a simple equation:

$$F = G \frac{m_1 m_2}{d^2}$$

F = force of gravity between two objects, m_1 and m_2 (newtons).
m_1 = mass (kilogrammes).
m_2 = mass (kilogrammes).
d = distance between the centre of the two masses (metres).
G = Universal gravitational constant (6.67 x 10^{-11} N-m^2/kg^2).

The greater the masses (m_1 and m_2), the greater the force of attraction between them, and the greater the distance (d), the weaker the force of attraction. It should be noted that the force weakens as an inverse-square law.

The inverse-square law is a law relating the intensity of an effect to the inverse square of the distance from the cause. Gravity follows an inverse-square law, as do the effects of electric, magnetic, light, sound and radiation phenomena. Since the force of gravity decreases as the square of the distance, a planet twice as far from the Sun is pulled toward the Sun with a quarter the force; three times as far, a ninth and four times as far, a sixteenth and so on. Thus the pull of gravity diminishes very quickly with distance.

To determine the mutual gravitational force on a person of mass 80 kg standing on the surface of the Earth at the equator.

$$F = G\, m_e m_o / d^2 \quad \text{or} \quad F = ma$$

Where,

Mass of Earth (m_e) = 5.98 x 10^{24} kilogrammes.
Radius of Earth (d) = 6.38 x 10^6 kilometres.
Mass of Body (m_o) = 80 kilogrammes.
G = 6.67 x 10^{-11} N-m^2/kg^2.
A = acceleration due to gravity = 9.80 m/s^2.

$$F = \frac{6.67 \times 10^{-11} \times 5.98 \times 10^{24} \times 80}{(6.38 \times 10^6)^2} \qquad\qquad F = ma = 80 \times 9.80$$
$$= 784 \text{ newtons}$$

$$= \frac{3191 \times 10^{13}}{40.70 \times 10^{12}}$$

$$= \textbf{784 newtons}$$

To determine the mutual gravitational force on a person of mass 80 kg on the International Space Station at an altitude of 400 kilometres.

Where,

Mass of Earth (m_e) = 5.98 x 10^{24} kilogrammes.
Radius of Earth (d) = 6.38 x 10^6 kilometres.
Altitude of ISS = 400 kilometres.
Mass of Body (m_o) = 80 kilogrammes.
G = 6.67 x 10^{-11} N-m^2/kg^2.

$$F = 6.67 \times 10^{-11} \times 5.98 \times 10^{24} \times 80 / (6.38 \times 10^6 + 400 \times 10^3)$$

$$= \textbf{694 newtons}$$

This is about **88 percent of the gravity exerted on a person of 80 kilogrammes on the Earth's surface.**

So why are the astronauts onboard the ISS weightless and floating about as the Earth's gravity at orbital height is almost as strong as on the Earth's surface?

The answer is because the astronauts and the ISS are in free fall and falling at almost the same rate as the acceleration due to gravity at almost 9.8 m/s^2.

To determine the mutual gravity between two persons on the Earth's surface

Where,

Person 1 = 80 kilogrammes.

Person 2 = 80 kilogrammes.

Separation between persons = 1 metre.

G = Universal gravitational constant (6.67 x 10^{-11} N-m^2/kg^2).

$$F = 6.67 \times 10^{-11} \times 80 \times 80/1$$

$$= 42688 \times 10^{-11}$$

$$= \mathbf{0.43 \times 10^{-6} \, newtons}$$

Mutual Gravitational Attraction of Sun, Earth and Moon

To calculate the mutual force of gravity between the Sun and the Earth; then of the Earth and the Moon.

Mutual force of gravity between the Sun and the Earth.

Thus we have:

Mass (m_s) of Sun = 1.99 x 10^{30} kilogrammes.
Mass (m_e) of Earth = 6 x 10^{24} kilogrammes.
Mean distance (d) Sun to Earth = 1.50 x 10^{11} m.
Gravitational constant (G) = (6.67 x 10^{-11} N-m^2/kg^2).

$$F = G \, m_s m_e / d^2$$

$$= \frac{6.67 \times 10^{-11} \times 1.99 \times 10^{30} \times 6 \times 10^{24}}{(1.50 \times 10^{11})^2}$$

$$= \frac{6.67 \times 10^{-11} \times 11.4 \times 10^{54}}{2.25 \times 10^{22}}$$

$$= \mathbf{3.4 \times 10^{22} \text{ newtons}}$$

Mutual force of gravity between the Earth and the Moon.

We have:

Mass (m_e) of Earth = 6 x 10^{24} kilogrammes.
Mass (m_m) of Moon = 7.350 x 10^{22} kilogrammes.
Mean distance (d) Earth to Moon = 3.84 x 10^8 kilometres.
Gravitational constant (G) = (6.67 x 10^{-11} N-m^2/kg^2).

$$F = G \, m_e m_m / d^2$$

$$= \frac{6.67 \times 10^{-11} \times 6 \times 10^{24} \times 7.350 \times 10^{22}}{(3.84 \times 10^8)^2}$$

$$= \mathbf{0.019 \times 10^{22} \text{ newtons}}$$

To summarise:

Mutual force between Earth and Sun = 3.4×10^{22} newtons.

Mutual force between Earth and Moon = 0.019×10^{22} newtons.

Thus the mutual gravitational force between the Earth and the Sun is approximately **180 times** (3.4/0.0199) greater than the mutual gravitational force between the Earth and the Moon.

Mutual force of gravity between a person of 80 kg mass standing on the surface of the Sun, and Moon.

Sun

Mass (m_s) of Sun = 1.99×10^{30} kilogrammes.
Mass (m_p) of Person = 80 kilogrammes.
Radius of Sun (d) = 6.96×10^{8} m.
Gravitational constant (G) = $(6.67 \times 10^{-11}$ N-m^2/kg$^2)$.

$$F = G \, m_s m_p / d^2$$

$$= \frac{6.67 \times 10^{-11} \times 1.99 \times 10^{30} \times 80}{(6.96 \times 10^{8})^2}$$

$$= \frac{1013.84 \times 10^{19}}{48.44 \times 10^{16}}$$

$$= \mathbf{20.93 \times 10^3 \ newtons}$$

Moon

Mass (m_m) of Moon = 7.36×10^{22} kilogrammes.
Mass (m_p) of Person = 80 kilogrammes.
Radius of Moon (d) = 1.74×10^{6} m.
Gravitational constant (G) = $(6.67 \times 10^{-11}$ N-m^2/kg$^2)$.

$$F = \frac{6.67 \times 10^{-11} \times 7.36 \times 10^{22} \times 80}{(1.74 \times 10^{6})^2}$$

$$= \frac{3927.3 \times 10^{11}}{3.03 \times 10^{12}}$$

$$= 130 \text{ newtons}$$

To summarise:

A person with a mass of 80 kilogrammes would experience different gravitational forces when standing on the surface of the following celestial bodies:

Sun: 21,000 newtons

Earth: 784 newtons

Moon: 130 newtons

Thus the gravitational force on a person or body on the surface of the Moon is 1/6 to that of the surface of the Earth: (130/784 = 1/6). Whilst the gravitational force of a person or body on the surface of the Sun is 27 times greater than on the surface of the Earth:

$$21000/784 = \mathbf{27}$$

Gravitational attraction the Moon has upon a person of mass 80 kilogrammes, standing on the Earth's surface.

Mass (m_m) of Moon = 7.36×10^{22} kilogrammes.
Mass (m_p) of Person = 80 kilogrammes.
Mean distance (d) Earth to Moon = 3.84×10^8 m.

$$F = G \, m_m m_p / d^2$$

~ 78 ~

$$= \frac{6.67 \times 10^{-11} \times 7.36 \times 10^{22} \times 80}{(3.84 \times 10^8)^2}$$

$$= \frac{3927 \times 10^{11}}{14.75 \times 10^{16}}$$

$$= 2.66 \times 10^{-3} \text{ newtons}$$

Gravitational attraction of the Sun has upon a person of mass 80 kilogramme, standing on the Earth's surface.

Mass (m_s) of Sun: 1.99×10^{30} kilogrammes.
Mass (m_p) of Person: 80 kilogrammes.
Mean distance (d) Sun to Earth: 1.50×10^{11} m.

$$F = \frac{6.67 \times 10^{-11} \times 1.99 \times 10^{30} \times 80}{(1.5 \times 10^{11})^2}$$

$$= \frac{1062 \times 10^{19}}{2.25 \times 10^{22}}$$

$$= 472 \times 10^{-3}$$

$$= 0.47 \text{ newtons}$$

In summary:

A person of 80 kilogrammes on the Earth's surface will experience:

Moon and 80 kg person = **0.0026 newtons.**
The Sun and 80 kg person = **0.47 newtons.**
The Earth and 80 kg person = **784 newtons**, (See note below).

Note: In the case of the Earth the force of attraction has been calculated using $f = mg = 784$ newtons.

From the above it can be seen that the Earth has the greatest attraction on a person on its surface. The results, when considering the mass of the Sun to the Moon and their respective distances from the Earth, demonstrate the power of the inverse-square law.

It can clearly be seen that the greater the mass of two bodies then the greater the mutual attraction between them, but also how distance between two masses demonstrates the inverse-square law.

The Earth's gravity dominates everywhere such that the mutual gravitation between two 80 kg people just 1 metre apart is infinitely small at 0.43 millionth of a newton – so imagine the magnitude of the Earth's gravity on that of the oceans – Earth's gravity is King!

Acceleration Due to Gravity (g)

Acceleration due to Gravity (g) is the acceleration of a free falling object under the effect of the Earth's gravitational field. Its value near the Earth's surface is about 9.8 metres per second each second.

Thus we can derive an expression that shows how the acceleration due to gravity varies with distance from the centre of the Earth at points exterior to the Earth's surface:

$$F = G \, m_e m_o / d^2$$

$$F = m_o g$$

Where,

m_e = mass of the Earth (6×10^{24} kilogrammes).
m_o = mass of object (Kilogrammes).
d = distance between object and centre of the Earth (metres).

r = radius of the Earth (6.38×10^6 metres).
G = Universal gravitational constant (6.67×10^{-11} N-m^2/kg^2).
g = acceleration due to gravity on Earth (9.8 m/s^2).

Thus we have,

$m_o g = G \, m_e \, m_o / d^2$

$g = G \, m_e / d^2$

Therefore an object 6,000 kilometres above the Earth's surface would accelerate (g) at:

$$g = 6.67 \times 10^{-11} \times 6.0 \times 10^{24} / (6.38 \times 10^6 + 6.0 \times 10^6)^2$$

$$= 4.02 \times 10^{14} / (1.238 \times 10^7)^2$$

$$= \textbf{2.60 m/s}^2$$

Gravity attracts all objects that have mass towards the centre of the Earth and the attraction diminishes very quickly, obeying the inverse square law as an object leaves the Earth's surface towards space. The acceleration due to gravity at the Earth's surface is 9.8 m/s^2.

At the equator, a person weighing 80 kilogrammes is experiencing the same motion as the Earth's rotation, that is, a speed of 1,675 km/h (about 1,040 mph) tangentially to the Earth's surface. So a reasonable question to ask is why does the Earth's rotation not fling this body off into space?

The answer is due to the Earth's gravity. The 80 kilogramme body will have a force of 784 newtons acting upon it (see calculation earlier in this appendix) and holding the body to the surface of the Earth. The reality being that it is inertia (the tendency of mass, our bodies, to continue moving in a straight line) being overcome by the Earth's gravity that keeps a person bound to the surface of the planet.

It should be clearly understood that if the inertia was such to overcome gravity by the Earth spinning much more rapidly about its axis, then the body would be flung off into space as a tangent to the surface of the planet – the body would NOT be flung upwards.

To determine the escape speed (velocity) from the Earth

$v_e = \sqrt{2Gm/r}$

Where,

$G = 6.67 \times 10^{-11}$ N-m^2/kg^2).
$M = 5.98 \times 10^{24}$ kilogrammes.
$R = 6.38 \times 10^6$ metres.

$v_e = \sqrt{2 \times 6.673 \times 10^{-11} \times 5.98 \times 10^{24}} \quad = \sqrt{125.1 \times 10^6}$

  = 11.2 m/s

Escape speed

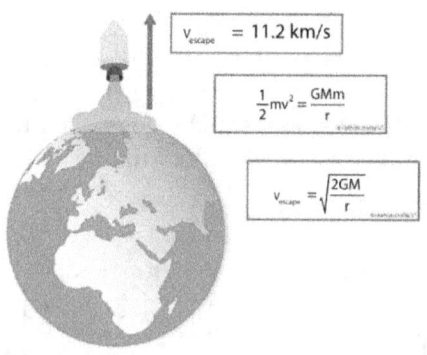

$V_{escape} = 11.2$ km/s

$\frac{1}{2}mv^2 = \frac{GMm}{r}$

$V_{escape} = \sqrt{\frac{2GM}{r}}$

Appendix 3

CENTRIPETAL and CENTRIFUGAL FORCE

It should be abundantly clear that a centripetal force is not a separate force such as a gravitational force, magnetic force or indeed a piece of string, but simply a generic name for any force that causes an object to follow a circular path such as the Earth's gravity keeping the International Space Station in orbit, or a piece of string connected to a ball that you are whirling about your head. Perhaps a less confusing term would be centripetal effect!

By the same token a centrifugal force is a fictitious force in that the term is applied to an outward force attributed to circular motion, and again a less confusing term would be centrifugal effect.

The equation for centripetal or centripetal force (F):

$$F = m \, v^2/r$$

Where,

F = centripetal or centrifugal force in newtons.
m = mass in kilogrammes.
v = velocity in metres per second.
r = radius in metres.

To determine the centripetal force of an iron ball of mass 25 kg being swung in a circle of radius 8 metres at a speed of 12 metres per second.

$F = 25 \times 12^2/8 = $ **450 newtons**

The lesson from this example is that the string prevented the iron ball flying away at a tangent to the circle as it exerted a centre seeking force on the ball. Cut the string and the ball flies away – a science teacher will tell you that a centripetal force acted on the ball, but this is misleading as there is no such thing as a centripetal force; the words centripetal force are a generic term that applies to any force that keeps a moving object flying in a circle – gravity being a perfect example, in keeping the Moon from flying off into space, or the Earth in orbit around the Sun.

To determine the centripetal force to keep Susan on a Fun Fare merry-go-round

Where,

Susan's mass = 32 kilogrammes.
Susan's tangential velocity = 2.35 m/s^2.
Diameter of merry-go-round = 3 metres.

$F = mv^2/r = 32 \times 2.352/1.5 =$ **118 newtons**

Thus Susan will need to exert a force of 118 newtons to stay on the merry-go-round; otherwise she will be flung off tangentially at a speed of 2.35 metres per second.

To determine the centrifugal force on a person of mass 80 kg standing on the surface of the Earth at the equator.

$$F = mv^2/r \quad \text{or } F = ma$$

Where,

F = centripetal or centrifugal force in newtons.
m = mass of person = 80 kilogrammes.
v = velocity of Earth at the equator = 465 metres/second.
r = radius of Earth at the equator = 6.38 x 10^6 metres.
a = centrifugal acceleration = 0.034 m/s^2.

$F = 80 \times 465^2/6.38 \times 10^6$ $F = 80 \times 0.034$

$= 12.54 \times 216225 \times 10^{-6}$ $= \textbf{2.72 newtons}$

$= 12.54 \times 0.22 = \textbf{2.72 newtons}$

Now we know the mutual gravitational attraction of a person of 80 kilogrammes is 784 newtons to the Earth's surface, whilst the centrifugal force on the same person is just 2.72 newtons. This obviously means the Earth's gravity is 288 times stronger than the centrifugal force. The oceans have much more mass than a person of 80 kilogrammes, so how can such a weak force overcome the Earth's gravity and be the cause a tidal bulge – the simple answer is that it cannot.

To determine the centrifugal acceleration at the Earth's equator.

$$a = v^2/r$$

Where,

a = centrifugal acceleration in metres per second per second.
V = velocity of Earth at the equator = 465 metres per second.
R = radius of the Earth at the equator = 6.38 a 10^6 metres.

$a = 465^2/6.38 \times 10^6 = 216225/6.38 \times 10^6 = \textbf{0.034 m/s}^2$

We now see that centrifugal force at the equator is 0.034 m/s^2 whereas the acceleration due to gravity is 9.81 m/s^2. Again there is no contest - the Earth's acceleration due to gravity is (again) 288 times greater than the centrifugal acceleration.

Appendix 4

INERTIA, WEIGHT and SQUEEZING MASS

Inertia

Newton's first law (Principle of Inertia) states that every body preserves its state of rest or its state of uniform motion in a straight line, except in so far as it is made to change that state by external forces. Now every material object possesses inertia: how much depends on the amount of matter in the substance of the object. Inertia (inertial force) is measured in newtons within the metric system, (it should be noted that in the imperial system the unit of force was measured in pounds). We frequently meet examples of the inertia of matter in daily life. If you are standing up in a train, which suddenly starts to move forward you fall backwards because some force urged your feet forward. But the upper part of you, not being acted upon by a force, tended to remain still. If you are standing up in a moving train, which suddenly stops you fall forward for a similar reason. Jumping off a moving bus in the same direction as the bus is moving can be deemed dangerous, unless you deliberately throw your body backward, in order to land in a forward slanting position when you reach the ground.

The inertia of a flywheel keeps an engine running smoothly. Some bodies have more inertia than others; in other words, it is more difficult to start them from rest or stop them in motion. It is easier to push a small car rather than a lorry along a level road; the reason for this is because there is a greater quantity of matter in the lorry than in the small car. In other words the mass of the lorry is greater. This is not to be confused with the weight of the lorry as we are not trying to *lift* it.

The relation between force, mass and acceleration may be expressed algebraically as follows:

$$F = ma$$

Where F = force in newtons.
m = mass in kilogrammes.
a = acceleration in metres per second per second.

Weight

The downward force that results from the gravitational attraction of the Earth to bodies on its surface is called weight. It is directly proportional to the mass of the body and the mass of the Earth, decreasing inversely proportional to the square of their distance apart. To put it more succinctly weight is the 'force acting upon an object due to gravity'. Thus an astronaut will experience different weights on celestial bodies of different mass. For example, on the Moon, which has less mass than the Earth, the gravitational force is only 1/6 as strong as on the Earth. Thus a person weighing 80 kilogrammes on Earth, will only weigh approximately 13 kilogrammes on the Moon.

Weight is measured in newtons, where 1 newton is the force required to accelerate 1 kilogramme at 1 metre per second per second. The unit is named after Sir Isaac Newton (1642 – 1727). It should be noted that in 'everyday usage' weight really refers to the mass of a person or object. That is why people, when asked their weight, reply in kilogrammes, (or stones, pounds and ounces).

The difference between mass and weight must be clearly understood. Weight will vary dependent upon the mass of the bodies. On more massive planets astronauts weigh more than on less massive celestial bodies. Weight is a force. But the mass of the astronaut (unless he has been on a diet) will remain the same. Mass is the quantity of matter in a material body. The astronaut offers the same resistance to speeding up or slowing down regardless of whether the Earth, Moon, or anything at all is attracting him.

For example: In a spaceship located at a point between the Earth and the Moon, where gravitational forces cancel each other, the astronaut still has mass - if he were to stand on a scale, he would not weigh anything, but his resistance to a change in motion is the same as on Earth. As a further example it must be recognised that it would take the same push (effort) to start moving a vehicle on a level surface on the Moon as it would on the Earth, but it would require much more effort to lift the vehicle on Earth that it would on the Moon. The extra effort is required because of lifting the vehicle against the force of gravity. Mass and weight are very different from each other.

We have stated that the relation between force, mass and acceleration may be expressed algebraically as:

$$F = ma$$

Therefore in determining the weight of a body we may use the following formula:

$$W = mg$$

Where W = weight in newtons
m = mass of body in kilogrammes
g = acceleration due to the Earth's gravity (9.8 m/s^2).

As an example we can use the above formula to calculate the weight of a 1 kilogramme mass when it is on the surface of the Earth:

$$W = 1 \times 9.8$$

= 9.80 newtons

Thus a mass of 1 kilogramme will have a weight (force) of 9.8 newtons (2.2 pounds) acting upon it at the surface of the Earth due to gravity.

To determine the weight of a 60 kilogramme person on the surface of the Earth

W = 60 x 9.8 = **589 newtons**

Or,

Mass of Earth (m_e) = 5.98 x 10^{24} kilogrammes.
Radius of Earth (d) = 6.38 x 10^6 kilometres.
Mass of Body (m_o) = 60 kilogrammes.
G = 6.67 x 10^{-11} N-m^2/kg^2.

F = 6.67 x 10^{-11} x 5.98 x 10^{24} x 60/ (6.38 x 10^6)

= **589 newtons**

The Earth's gravitation exerts a 589 N force on a 60 kg person due to its gravitational field. Please note that in our everyday language, we do not say a person weighs 589 newtons, but weighs 60 kg

The Effect of Squeezing Mass

Weight is a variable force depending upon the amount of matter contained in an object. We will now consider a *thought experiment* and examine what happens to the Earth and objects on its surface when the Earth is squeezed down to a smaller size. Consider an ingot of gold on the Earth's surface weighing 100 kilogrammes. Standing next to the gold ingot is the owner who weighs 80 kilogrammes.

Now let us imagine we can shrink the Earth down to a quarter of its original size. Suddenly we find that the owner (body) of the gold ingot is much heavier. To our amazement we discover the body now weighs a staggering 1,280 kilogramme when placed on a weighing scale! Our amazement for the increase in body weight is only mitigated when we weigh the gold ingot and find it also has increased in weight to 1,600 kilogrammes - the owner may be heavier but he or she is that much richer..!

So what has happened?

The mean radius of the Earth is 6,370 kilometres and by shrinking it to a quarter of its original size we have reduced the mean radius to 1,593 kilometres. The mass of the Earth is the same but now contained in a smaller space.

Now if we magically elevate the gold ingot and the body to a point above the Earth where the surface used to be, we have another surprise. Assuming we can also weigh the gold ingot and body - we find the weight of the body and that of the gold ingot has returned to what it was before we shrank the Earth.

An application of Newton's law of Universal Gravitation and the inverse-square law easily explain this phenomenon. Shrinking the Earth down to a quarter of its original size whilst maintaining its mass has brought any object on its surface that much nearer to the geometric centre of the Earth. As gravity alters inversely proportional the square of the distance separating any two masses it follows that by shrinking the planet to a quarter of its original size we are that much nearer the geometric centre of the Earth for the same mass. In fact the objects are *four times nearer* which means they are *sixteen times heavier* - The following is the mathematical verification:

Weight of Gold Ingot on the Surface of the Earth before Shrinking the Earth.

Mass of Earth $(m_e) = 6.0$ x 10^{24} kilogrammes.
Radius of Earth $(d) = 6.38$ x 10^3 kilometres (approximately).
Mass of Gold ingot $(m_g) = 100$ kilogrammes.
Gravitational constant $(G) = (6.67$ x 10^{-11} N-m^2/kg^2).

$$F = G\, m_e\, m_g / d^2$$

$$= 6.67 \times 10^{-11} \times 6.0 \times 10^{24} \times 100/ (6.38 \times 10^3 \times 10^3)^2$$

$$= \textbf{983 newtons}$$

Weight of Body on the Surface of the Earth before Shrinking the Earth.

Mass of Earth $(m_e) = 6.0 \times 10^{24}$ kilogrammes.
Radius of Earth $(d) = 6.38 \times 10^3$ kilometres.
Mass of Body $(m_o) = 80$ kilogrammes.
Gravitational constant $(G) = (6.67 \times 10^{-11}$ N-m^2/kg^2).

$$F = G\ m_e m_o/d^2$$

$$= 6.67 \times 10^{-11} \times 6.0 \times 10^{24} \times 80/ (6.38 \times 10^3 \times 10^3)^2$$

$$= \textbf{787 newtons}$$

Weight of Gold Ingot on Surface of the Earth after Earth has shrunk.

Mass of Earth $(m_e) = 6.0 \times 10^{24}$ kilogrammes.
Radius of shrunken Earth $(d) = 1.595 \times 10^3$ kilometres, $(6.38 \times 10^3/4)$.
Mass of Gold ingot $(m_g) = 100$ kilogrammes.
Gravitational constant $(G) = (6.67 \times 10^{-11}$ N-m^2/kg^2).

$$F = G\ m_e\ m_g/d^2$$

$$= 6.67 \times 10^{-11} \times 6.0 \times 10^{24} \times 100 / (1.595 \times 10^3 \times 10^3)^2$$

$$= \textbf{15,731 newtons}$$

Weight of Body on the Surface of the Earth after the Earth has shrunk.

Mass of Earth (m_e) = 6.0 x 10^{24} kilogrammes.
Radius of shrunken Earth (d) = 1.595 x 10^3 kilometres.
Mass of Body (m_o) = 80 kilogrammes.
Gravitational constant (G) = (6.67 x 10^{-11} N-m^2/kg^2).

$$F = G\ m_e m_o / d^2$$

$$= 6.67 \times 10^{-11} \times 6.0 \times 10^{24} \times 80/ (1.595 \times 10^3 \times 10^3)^2$$

= 12,584 newtons

Therefore in summarising, we see that the weight of the gold ingot of a mass of 100 kilogrammes was 983 newtons, before the Earth was shrunk to a quarter of its original size. The weight of the gold ingot then increased dramatically to 15,731 newtons (a factor of 16) on the surface of the Earth after it had been shrunk to a quarter of its original size. The body (owners) weight also increased from 787 newtons to 12,584 newtons, a factor of 16 again. This compares to a factor of 4 for the distance – the difference between the surface and the centre of the Earth at normal size to that of the shrunken Earth.

It should be clearly understood that although the physical size of the Earth was reduced, the amount of matter (mass) remained the same. The Universal Gravitational equation also confirmed that if the gold ingot and the owner were transported to a point above the Earth where the surface used to be; we would find the weight of the owner and that of the gold ingot had returned to what it was before we shrank the Earth. The calculations clearly show that apart from the effect on the weight of a body when mass is squeezed into a smaller space, but also how significantly the force of gravity *diminishes* with distance. This is a good example of the 'power' of the inverse-square law and its exponential characteristic.

Appendix 5

Barycentre

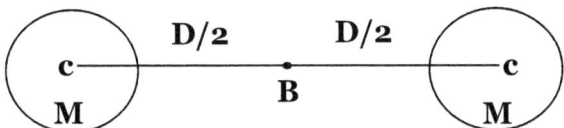

The position (B) is the barycentre for the two bodies (stars) of identical Mass (M). Both these bodies will orbit this point (B) and are separated by the same distances, D/2. Where D is the distance between the centres (c) of the two masses.

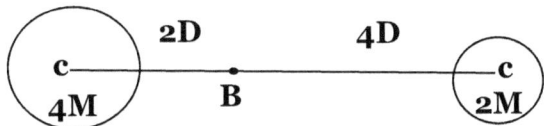

Now if one body is twice as massive (4M) as the other (2M), then the two bodies will orbit a centre of mass (B) one third of the distance between the centre of the stars as shown above. The larger bodies orbital motion will be less than the smaller body.

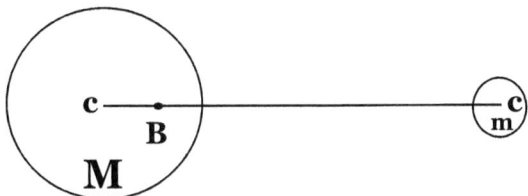

If one body (M) is much more massive than the other (m), then the two bodies will orbit a centre of mass (B) within the larger body as shown above. The larger bodies orbital motion will be far less than the smaller body.

Appendix 6

Free Fall

Free fall is a state of falling free from air resistance and other forces except for gravity. A falling object (mass) accelerates toward the Earth because of the gravitational force of attraction between the object and the Earth. The force of gravity that acts on an object we call the weight of the object.

We are all aware of the sensation we have in an elevator, if it is rising fast we can detect the pressure or force on our feet by the floor of the elevator. But if it is falling rapidly we will experience a lightness of feeling with perhaps an uncomfortable feeling in our stomach. These are due to the effects of acceleration and deceleration.

If we take this a step further and imagine you are in a box similar to an elevator high above the surface of the Earth; in fact the box is in space but still within the influence of the Earth's gravitational field. If the base or floor of the box is facing toward the Earth and the box is stationary with respect to the Earth's surface your senses will detect a force holding you to the base of the box. This you will assume is natural and due to gravity.

Should this box suddenly plummet towards the Earth as fast as falling objects accelerate towards the Earth (at an acceleration of 9.8 metres per second per second), then you will suddenly find you have no weight. If you push against the floor you will find yourself floating about in the box like a feather in the wind. You are now in a state of free fall, but note the Earth's gravity has not diminished and the reason you are floating is because your downward acceleration matches the acceleration due to gravity.

If the box plummeted towards the Earth with a far higher acceleration, then you would find yourself pressed toward the inner surface of the box furthest from the Earth; that is, the ceiling of the box – the ceiling becomes the floor.

The experience of being in free fall (zero gravity) is amply shown in videos on YouTube when the late Professor Stephen Hawkins, Professor of Mathematics, Cambridge University, became the first person with a disability to experience weightlessness in a zero-gravity inducing flight in 2007. The professor flew in a modified Boeing 727 which after climbing to about 33,000 feet, then descended rapidly for about 8,000 feet and for the next 20-30 seconds everything in the aircraft is weightless. A similar aircraft is used by NASA to train astronauts. The usually fit and young NASA astronauts involved often refer to their own zero-gravity aircraft as the Vomit Comet, because of the regularity with which they lose their lunch to its stomach-churning manoeuvres.

Taking this explanation a little further imagine you are in a stationary spaceship, with no means to see outside, far out in inter-galactic space and far from any gravitational body. Since the spaceship is at rest and there is no gravitational body to influence your environment, you will be in a state of weightlessness since weight is what you call the force with which a large mass pulls on an object.

Thus you will find yourself bobbing and floating about the spaceship.

Now when the spaceship starts to accelerate in the forward direction relative to the distant stars, you will find yourself pushed back towards the rear of the spaceship. You will, in a sense, have a force of gravity. Now when the spacecraft decelerates, you will find yourself thrust forward in the same way that people are in any conveyance, which is speeding up or slowing down on Earth. When the spaceship comes to rest again you find yourself bobbing and floating about again. Your body and brain will tell you (from your everyday experience of motion) that the spacecraft was initially motionless, then started to move forward, then slowed down and stopped.

To continue with this theme let us imagine you and a number of fellow space passengers are now travelling along in a spaceship with a constant velocity relative to the distant stars. Suddenly a stray and massive celestial body narrowly misses the rear of your spaceship, but inside the spaceship nobody is aware of the near miss, as there are no windows to look out.

In this example the passengers will feel they are being pulled back into their seats as the celestial body passes them by -the mass of the passing body has imparted a force on them - but since they were not aware of the presence of the celestial body and since the effect is the same as if the spaceship had accelerated, all the passengers will assume the spaceship had accelerated and carry on with whatever they were doing before the event. Thus the passengers have no way of determining whether they are being subject to an acceleration or being attracted by a gravitational field – this is Einstein's principle of equivalence which states that observations made in an accelerated reference frame are indistinguishable from observations made in a Newtonian gravitational field.

OTHER BOOKS BY THE AUTHOR

21ST CENTURY ELECTRICITY
(Foreword by David Bellamy OBE)
ISBN 978-1-78507-390-8

Obtainable from Amazon, W H Smiths and New Generation
Publishing

COUNTDOWN TO OBLIVION
ISBN 141202685-7

Trafford Publishing
www.trafford.com
E-mail sales: sales@trafford.com

Also obtainable from Amazon

KINDLE cartoon books

I just love my computer

Computer Rage

Romans, Greeks, Egyptians and Gauls

Aliens and Space

KINDLE fantasy book for children

Troll Castle and the Forbidden Chamber of Gold

THE AUTHOR

The author is a retired telecommunications engineering manager, who was employed for almost forty years with a large telecommunications organisation - qualifications consist of a National Certificate in Electrical Engineering and a Full Technological Certificate (Telecommunications) which included a distinction in digital computing at year five; many years ago a member of the Institute of Electrical and Electronic Technician Engineers (IEETE).

Hobbies include amateur astronomy (member of the Shropshire Astronomical Society), gardening, reading, DIY, travelling, computing, amateur radio (certificate to qualify transmitting and receiving on FM only), a passionate love and appreciation of coastal and country walking.

During his early years as a member of the Youth Hostels Association (YHA) the author completed the YHA (7 peaks) 40 mile marathon walk which entailed climbing the seven highest peaks in South Wales, starting at 0500 hrs from the Llanddeusant Youth Hostel in the Black Mountains, Carmarthenshire, crossing and climbing the Brecon Beacons, and completing the marathon the same day at approximately 2200 hrs at the George VI Memorial Youth Hostel, Capel-y-Ffin, Black Mountains near Hay-on-Wye.

The author had a power boat moored in the Teifi Estuary for a number of years, and when at sea, he and his wife enjoyed the beautiful Welsh coastal scenery, mackerel and pollack fishing, seal watching and being enchanted by the inquisitive approach and playful 'showing off' by the dolphins in Cardigan Bay.

www.ingramcontent.com/pod-product-compliance
Lightning Source LLC
Chambersburg PA
CBHW060423290526
45791CB00002B/852